The Great Little
Book of Happiness

"A Guide to Leading a Happier Life"

The Great Little
Book of Happiness

"A Guide to Leading a Happier Life"

Andrew Marshall

First published 2008 by Radiant Sun Books

30 Haywood Grange
Little Haywood
Stafford
ST18 0UB

www.radiantsunbooks.com

ISBN 978-0-9559364-0-1

A CIP catalogue record for this book is available from the British Library.

Cover Artwork by Judith Turner

Typeset in Calisto MT 10.5pt

Prepared and printed by:
York Publishing Services Ltd
64 Hallfield Road
Layerthorpe
York YO31 7ZQ
Tel: 01904 431213
Website: www.yps-publishing.co.uk

Contents

Introduction

Although we live in a society that has the greatest wealth and material standards it has ever enjoyed, there is a distinct malaise. This malaise is a lack of genuine happiness and fulfilment, a lack of inner peace and a lack of stability. Some cultures with considerably less material wealth than ours may marvel at the technological advancements and living conditions we have but are bemused at the apparent almost total absence of spiritual foundation or values. As a society, we come close to Oscar Wilde's cynic: we know the price of everything but the value of nothing.

Politicians and successive governments have tried in vain to restore the missing quality by imposing standards in education and other areas of life but haven't succeeded because the problem is not one of outer values but of consciousness. If we want to enjoy quality of life and the richness and abundance of the present moment, we have to take responsibility for our own state of consciousness and do something about it. For certain, no-one else is going to do it for us.

This book is intended as an aid to restoring inner fulfilment and making life happier. To begin with, we look at the causes of unhappiness and of its opposite, happiness. Then progressively we dismantle the obstructions to happiness and build the causes or conditions that lead to a joyful, happier life. Happiness, as we shall see, is a state of mind and this book contains the essentials for bringing about a fresh state of mind.

To lead a happy life does not require luck or money. To do the things in this book will cost you nothing except the price of the book – not even that if you have borrowed it – and a little time. All that is required is a little thought and some application. If you truly follow the things suggested, life will become richer, more fulfilling and happier.

Some things may challenge you because there is a need to overcome some old habits of thinking and create new ones but everything in this book works. Everything has been tried and tested. The fundamental principles are as old as time – some from what is sometimes called 'ancient wisdom' – but the approach we will be taking is for the modern age. All the techniques and exercises have been used on courses and workshops run by the author and his wife for many years. You can just read the book without doing them but then that's rather like looking through a travel brochure and not going anywhere. Some people are like that – they just read, listen or watch but don't actually do anything. I hope you, on the other hand, will travel far.

Please enjoy the book and enjoy working through it.

1

Why isn't everyone happy?

Why the mind is master of our happiness

It's sad but it's true: most people, most of the time, are not happy. A human being is a miracle of nature. Faces should light up when one miracle sees another one, but usually they don't. Look around you when you walk down the street or are in a crowd. How many smiling faces do you see? Our streets are full of apparition-like people, corpse-like almost, carrying serious or vacant expressions with minds anywhere but in the true joy of the present moment. Life shouldn't be like that. Looking and hoping for lasting happiness and blaming anything and everything from the weather to the government for not providing it, we seem to have become a race of malcontents. Why?

The master or controller of our happiness and, just as importantly, the absence of it, isn't our state of wealth or even our health, nor is it our employment or lack of it nor our social status nor anything else in our environment. Of course, these things will play a part but people can be relatively poor and can even have poor health, yet still have a twinkle in their eyes or a smile on their lips. Each of us knows, deep down, that happiness has to come from inside and the controller of that is simply one thing: the mind.

Your mind is the controller of your happiness and my mind is the controller of my happiness; it really is that simple. But our minds are very complex. It takes a great deal of effort to change the way we habitually think, feel and react – but we can and, when we do, we control the controller; we become the masters of our lives and our happiness. Rather than being slaves to the whims of the mind, we can make the mind our servant.

Each one of us has, since birth, built up a complex and convoluted storehouse or "library" of likes, dislikes, loves, hates, fears, judgments, prejudices and so on which cause us to think, feel, speak and react in a certain way. In other words, we are conditioned. Everything we see, hear, taste, touch, feel and think passes through and is affected by the contents of our library.

To gain mastery over ourselves, we need to bring in some extra light and different knowledge into our storehouse. We need to rebuild our conditioning. This doesn't involve dismantling the old, book by book, shelf by shelf and brick by brick. We don't have to analyse every thought and feeling that arises; but we do need to see things, and ourselves, in a different way. When we look at things differently, gradually our preconceptions about many things change. Negative emotions, those clouds that cast shadows across our faces, start to dissolve and appear far less often. We become happier, more contented.

This isn't something that happens overnight, of course. It is a journey that can be challenging at times but there is also a great deal of fun and satisfaction to be had. This book is intended as a guide-book for the trip. Please use it to check where you are and where you might be going – but any guide book is limited. The real journey and scenery you have to make and discover for yourself!

Why our world is nothing but "shifting sands"

One of the basic causes of unhappiness is dependence on things in the outside world for our stability and well-being and not accepting that absolutely everything is in a perpetual state of change. That comes very close to home in the guise of our own body. As a child or a teenager, we may have looked forward to looking older but that anticipation doesn't last for very long once we reach adulthood, does it? Most of us don't relish the idea of aging at all and we try to hang onto our youthful looks, suppleness, fitness and so on for as long as we possibly can. I failed on that one some time ago! But seriously, there is in all of us, or nearly all of us, a dread of becoming old and frail, perhaps incontinent, losing teeth, having failing hearing and eyesight and possibly mental faculties. The reason for this dread is that we have failed to embrace fully – and I mean really fully – the inevitability of change. No matter how hard we try, we cannot preserve the body, but there is still a sneaking wish to prolong it as long as possible. That's not unreasonable, don't get me wrong, but what happens is that instead of treating the body as an instrument that is ours to use for a limited length of time, we become dearly attached to it (or abhor it, which is equally as bad) and so it becomes a source of unhappiness as it deteriorates. It not only becomes a source of unhappiness, it also becomes a source of fear because it is not only aging that results in death; death can come at any time and the thought of some of the possible methods of its arrival, particularly cancer, terrorism, fire, drowning and so on, can lead to irrational fears which affect our thinking, our behaviour and, most importantly, our happiness factor.

If we can fully embrace our own impermanence, we can more easily embrace the vulnerability of everything in our world to the force of change. Unfortunately, it is human nature not to do that. Instead, we tend to see things as more or less there for good, as solid and real. That can make us miserable because we will then try to hang onto the "good" things – the ones that we see as essential to our happiness – and feel down when they start to slip away from us. The "bad" things will cast shadows over us because the fact that they will eventually go away is not something we have properly grasped. In fact, as we shall see later, there is neither good nor bad but while we continue to label things that way, the seeds of unhappiness are there.

The world is a marvellous teacher for producing things that shake us out of our stupor when we are taking things for granted and feeling comfortable with everything. Society is shaken time and time again by catastrophic events, either natural or manmade, and the degree of shock is dependent to a great degree on the extent to which our own world appears to have been violated or threatened. Day in, day out there are news reports of people in various parts of the world blowing other people up and committing all manner of atrocities. These tragedies are often only mentioned in passing – until one of them is close to home, in the country where we live, for instance. And isn't it the same in our individual lives? If news comes to us that a close friend or relative has been diagnosed with a life-threatening illness, it affects us not only because of the compassion we will feel towards that person and members of his or her family but it affects us also because the normality of our little world has changed. The person who has always been there may not be for much longer, and the closer they are to us, the stronger the emotional reaction is likely to be.

There are millions of examples you and I could no doubt think of where we would say that change, vulnerability and impermanence threaten our and others' state of happiness. But in fact we would be wrong. The reason we would be wrong is that the threat to our happiness doesn't lie in those things that are going to change. The cause is the way we *see* those things, or rather our failure to see things as they really are. We'll come back to this later.

A question of false identity – and how we cut ourselves off

"Just *who* do you think you are?" That was a question my parents would often ask me when I was a boy – not from any philosophical standpoint – just as a remonstration for something said or done that in their view amounted to mischief or cheek! Little did I know then that I would spend my adult life exploring that question. So let me ask you, very politely, "Who do you think *you* are? Who *are* you?"

The normal response to that type of question would be something along the lines of, "I'm Jim (or Alice or whatever our name happens to be," wouldn't it? That might be followed with a description of our occupation, where we live or any of our personal details. The fact is, though, that answer is false. Conventionally we have to say it and will always say it because we have to communicate in a world that is full of conventions; but it isn't right when we look at things in a deeper way than normal.

You might say to me, "Does it really matter when all we're looking at is happiness?" Well, yes it does matter because the most basic and fundamental threat to our own happiness is not who or what others think we are; it's who *we* think we are. We all see ourselves as separate human beings – individual, self-contained units – and as long as we see ourselves in this way, there will be things in this world to protect ourselves from. We will see danger "out there" to our peace and happiness. So what do we do? We build barriers, barriers of protection in our minds (and often physical barriers, too). The trouble is that these barriers affect our thinking, our feelings and our behaviour. They stop us engaging fully with our world and with ourselves.

Eventually, we have to overcome this mental picture that creates a false sense of identity or reality. At first, we have to start breaking down some of the mental walls by looking at things in a clearer and more logical way. In other words, we have to think through the falseness a little bit. We'll take a closer look at this in chapter 6. Later, we have to go beyond the thinking stage, usually through meditation, and experience a state that is beyond what we might call the "little I". But that's enough of this heady stuff for the moment. Let's look at something with a reputation that is better known, if not better in itself – the ego.

The ego – our friend and worst enemy

Arising from the basic sense of "I" is the ego. The ego is nothing other than a complex of mental constructs and beliefs about ourselves. There is no actual thing we can identify and say, "Hey, I've found an ego!" But the effect of it is so strong that we might be forgiven for thinking that it is something tangible.

The very word "ego" usually has some negative connotations. A person with a "big ego" is almost synonymous with "a big-head" and certain less polite variations. We all know the experience of suffering the company of someone who is puffed up with a sense of self-importance and we may even look back with embarrassment remembering times when we have been insufferable as well. The big-ego person is reinforcing the strength of the sense of "me" by building up a false picture of who he or she really is. Status is all-important to the big ego, whether that is measured as social standing, career success, material possessions or whatever.

So big egos are relatively easy to spot (actually, sometimes they are not but that's another story) and we might think, "Phew, thank goodness I haven't got one." But what about little egos? The truth of the matter is that we all have an ego and we would have great difficulty in society or in whatever environment we found ourselves without one. It is the ego that gives us a sense of self-esteem, a sense of worth, that commands how we interact with others and so forth. Without a society of egos, we would have no society. There would be no structure, no commerce, no transport, and no self-improvement. Why? Because it is the ego that has the sense of need and is the driver of all ambition, of our desires and our dreams.

"Ego", in the sense of self-esteem, governs how we see ourselves and consequently how much confidence we have. A person with low self-esteem isn't a happy person whereas a person with good self-esteem has confidence and is able to conduct himself or herself happily and confidently in the world. So the ego also has positive attributes because it is helps to create an integrated personality – up to a point. But there is a sting in the tail, a very poisonous sting.

Remember that the ego is something each one of us has created for ourselves. It is the strengthened sense of "I" which leads to a strong sense of "me" and "mine". So "I" have "my" property; "I" have "my" standards and reputation; "I" have "my" wants, feelings and emotions. That means "I" have things that can be lost, stolen, damaged or destroyed. "I" am vulnerable so "I" create a world around "me", an imaginary world with imaginary boundaries and, like a child playing games, "I" am convinced it is all real.

Until I doubt the reality of this world of mine, I go through life pursuing those things that will maintain and even strengthen my imaginary world. Things that threaten my world cause me fear or even anger; when things are lost, I bear disappointment and pain. But the ego cannot let up and cannot admit failure. It builds up new pictures, new desires that, when fulfilled, will make everything all right. Round and round we all go. And it does go on – on and on – until something within us begins to dawn: Uncle Ego isn't such a good guy after all. The games he has us playing aren't making us happy.

If we look at much of the hardship and suffering in the world we can see that. People blow each other up because "my" way of life, or "my" religion is the right way and everyone else is wrong. Crime in society is motivated by what "I" want. Tensions in families and workplaces arise because of conflicting wants and expectations of many "I's".

In short, it is the ego that gives rise to all our negative ways of thinking and our negative emotions such as pride, anger, hatred, jealousy, greed and so on.

Why seeking our own happiness is doomed to failure

Of course we want to be happy. Nobody wants to suffer. Seeking happiness is the most natural thing in the world. Everyone does it. If there is a choice of dishes on the menu at a restaurant, we don't choose the ones we don't like. Unless we are mentally or emotionally sick, we don't purposely inflict pain on ourselves. If our legs ache and there's a seat handy, we sit down. All these are simple things that flow naturally in life because that's the way life is; it's the natural tendency to move away from pain and discomfort to those things that make us comfortable and happy. But if our lives are driven by the intention of making ourselves happy, it isn't going to happen. At best, we might gain a superficial level of happiness but deep down it doesn't work. It can't work in a world where nothing is stable. There has to be an inner peace and contentment.

The problem with seeking happiness for ourselves is that inevitably it gives rise to a certain degree of selfishness. Our thoughts become focused on ourselves. We try to create a bubble around us that keeps unhappiness factors away and, perhaps unwittingly, we become very insular. "I am sorry you are unhappy but I'm afraid it's nothing to do with me," is the sort of outlook that can develop. Our hearts become tough and cold instead of warm and pliable. Inwardly we lose all sense of joy.

If we want to be truly happy and content, we have to be less concerned with "me". In fact, the more we are concerned with others' welfare and happiness, the happier we will become. In other words, we do the opposite of what Uncle Ego might think. It's a universal law and it works. When we take the focus away from ourselves, we take the focus off the things in life which we blame for .... well, blame for anything, really.

Some people have the gift of being able to see the energy fields around people and they will tell you that a generous, outward looking person has vibrant, outgoing energy. But you don't have to see that to know it. You can sense it. You know what it is like to be in the company of a warm-hearted person. On the other hand, the energy of a pleasure-seeking person is not something that most of us can put up with for very long. Their energy will deplete us after a while either because they are drawing on our energy or because their energy is rough and chaotic. Either way, they're exhausting. You know the sort of reaction people have: "X is a nice person – in small doses!"

Identifying our own happiness factors

Whether it is a throwback from more austere times that has conditioned them I don't know but many people seem to have a distinct reservation about being happy. It is almost as though they think that happiness is wrong and that they are not meeting their responsibility as human beings unless they feel and look glum. Many children, unfortunately, are brought up in families which are not happy and innocent joyfulness is very quickly lost. Whether we have had a sad or unhappy past or whether we simply mix with dour people, if we have dampened spirits we have to change the tendencies of the mind. Human beings are creatures of habit and the tendency of the mind is to make us repeat those thoughts, words and actions that maintain the status quo. In other words, we reinforce the way we always have been – unless we make a determined effort to change.

If you wish to be happier than you are now, you must have the will to do something about it and if you have any doubts as to whether it is right or responsible to be happier, let's start with the thought that a happier human being is a better human being. Remember that moods are infectious and happy people tend to uplift others.

A little exercise

A very useful exercise which I suggest you pause and do in a few moments is to identify those things in life that create a sense of joy and fulfilment within you. Just take a piece of paper or maybe a notebook and make a list. They may be quite small things and your list may be quite short to start with; that doesn't matter. Review the list from time to time and don't be frightened to cross things out or to add to it because you'll almost certainly have different thoughts on it as you progress. That's the first part of the exercise. The second part is to think *why* those things bring happiness and fulfilment and why some seem to do so more than others. Do actions which are more selfless in nature bring greater fulfilment than those that are motivated by selfishness, for example?

This list will prove to be a valuable learning tool over time so look after it. You will have to be completely honest with yourself for it to work well but the important thing is to highlight in your mind what actions, thoughts or words of yours have an uplifting effect on you. You will have the basis for increasing the quality of your life by knowing which areas need to be enhanced and so increase the tendency to do them. To put it another way, you will have equipped yourself for creating more causes for happiness in life.

Increasing our potential for happiness

This following exercise applies the old adage "energy follows thought". If you have worked with chi or done any other energy work, you will know how true that phrase is. If you haven't, don't worry – no experience is required! What we are going to do is a little visualisation, which simply means picturing something in the mind sufficiently strongly so that it has an effect. By doing this, we change the energy in our body temporarily. For example, if you are feeling hungry and picture in your mind sitting down to a favourite meal, you might notice that your mouth starts to water a little. Our exercise is a little bit more than that, though, because what we are going to do is not only to change the energy of the body (it should feel a little lighter) but more importantly it will raise the energy of our thinking and increase the potential for realising happiness. Remember that happiness is a state of mind – so it is important to sow seeds that can grow into happiness in rich, fertile soil.

- *Choose a place where you can sit quietly without being disturbed for a few minutes.*

- *Think of the things you have already identified as those that increase your happiness. Now visualise these things actually filling your life. Don't try to argue whether it is possible or not – that isn't the point. Simply allow a picture to arise in your mind where your life is filled with happiness and the things that cause happiness. Be happy with this and allow yourself to smile a little (or a lot!)*

- *Take about five minutes to do this, a little more if you wish.*

Was it a reasonably pleasant experience? It should have been and you should be feeling reasonably good after doing it. By doing this exercise easily and innocently, we push our mental boundaries outwards and sow the seeds for the blocks to happiness to dissolve. If there was any difficulty, don't worry about it. Try it again later. In fact, this isn't a one-off thing to do because the more we do it, the more effective it becomes. The important thing is not to strain and, if objections to doing it arise in your mind, just let them go. The ego will object from time to time, that's its nature, but just let it go.

How the law of cause and effect rules our lives

Tied in with the quest for deeper understanding, fulfilment and happiness is the amazing law of cause and effect.

Sometimes, particularly in a spiritual or quasi-spiritual context, the expression "law of karma" is used. "Karma" simply means action but is often used to imply the fruits or results of actions, whether one's own or someone else's. It's an expression that unfortunately is often misused and misunderstood, often leading to "deep and meaningful" discussions when often a straightforward explanation is all that is needed.

Simply stated, the law of cause and effect means that every effect, every set of circumstances, has its cause or causes. If I burn my hand on the oven door, for example, there are a number of causes that lead up to it, the simplest of which are my movements, the heat of the door and, almost certainly and most importantly, my lack of attention or co-ordination. On a grander scale, an earthquake has certain geological causes and so on. For physical events, the law is very easy to understand. Where we can often lose vision is in the application of the law in our own lives.

Nothing, absolutely nothing, in our present circumstances is without preceding causes. Things don't happen "just by chance" – there is *always* a reason. We might put certain events down to luck but luck or fortune, good, bad or indifferent, is simply the law of cause and effect taking its course. The word "simply" is perhaps an overstatement because cause and effect is incredibly complex and we'll need to have a deeper look at some of its implications later on; but let's just say for now that this law is inescapable. When we start to understand it better, we begin to realise that there is no use at all in blaming others (which is a favourite human pastime) for our predicaments or for our state of mind. We have to take responsibility and there's no copping out.

Why our every thought, word and action affects our state of happiness

My parents used to have many ways of trying to coax me to behave and tell the truth. Perhaps you, too, were told that spots on the tongue were a likely consequence of telling fibs. I have a vivid recollection of being told that we all have a soul that is normally white but has shadows and black spots on it from misdeeds. If that's true, goodness knows what mine looks like now but at the time I had an image in my mind of an amorphous white blob peppered with many dark bits, looking like a misshapen steamed suet pudding full of over-sized raisins and dried dates, floating somewhere above my head.

What they were saying in an oblique sort of way, though, was that all our actions and words have consequences and that those consequences impinge on our future happiness or spiritual well-being. That isn't a thought just for children – it applies, perhaps even more strongly, throughout our adult life.

The law of cause and effect says that every action, on every level, has consequences. That means that everything we do, everything we say, and indeed everything we think, is a seed that will have a future effect. Some of those seeds are weak and the consequences will be insignificant but others will obviously have more impact. Words said in anger, for instance, come out effortlessly and in an instant but can have dire and long-lasting effects. But what about thinking?

Whatever we think has an effect on our energy. When I say "energy", I don't mean the energy of "get up and go" necessarily although there can be an impact. Remember that our body is a complex energy field and through it is a network of subtle energy channels, the major ones being called meridians. This energy is sometimes called "chi". When our thinking is positive, the chi in our bodies is vibrant and flows well. Good and plentiful chi, as we might call it, results in vitality, well-being and a strong immune system.

We often say that someone "radiates good health" and it is true that there is a radiating of energy. Most of us can sense the energy radiating from someone to a degree. Now what happens when we have a negative thought? The energy changes, doesn't it? It withdraws. We can feel on top of the world and someone will say something and we "sink to our boots". It isn't the direct effect of what the other person says that causes the energy change but how we perceive it. To put it another way, we have a negative reaction. Our mind goes into a negative state and we don't feel good anymore.

That's an example of a clear immediate reaction but the effect of long-term negative thinking is disastrous. We become shrivelled or distorted inside. The chi stagnates causing congestion. Health suffers and our outlook on life is far from happy. This isn't from negative actions or even speech – just from thinking. My job for many years brought me into contact with people who had long-term negative thinking and behavioural problems and virtually all of them looked at least ten years older than their true age. The trouble is that once we start thinking in a certain way, it is difficult to stop. One thought creates (or causes) another thought and all of us have a history of a certain amount of negative thinking. That negative habit is so strong, sometimes like a current that is not obviously present from looking at the surface, that it becomes difficult to sustain a positive train of thought for long. Our energy, our chi, is in a poor state and later, if not earlier, in life our health will inevitably suffer.

Perhaps more often, our thinking isn't particularly positive or negative but is chaotic – all over the place. Most of us suffer from a case of "butterfly mind" at least some of the time. We think of one thing, then another; then we hear a sound or something said and we're off again. Or we're in the dentist's waiting room and pick up a magazine and our mind is distracted here, there and everywhere. What's happening to our energy? It's scattered, loose, and untidy. Our chi is incoherent; our energy field becomes weak and leaky. This is what happens when we are unfocused. Scattered thinking doesn't necessarily make us feel bad in the short-term but it depletes our energy reserves over a period of time and the only way to overcome it is to draw our thinking and our energy in. We'll look at this later in the book.

Good, positive, selfless thinking will sow seeds for a happier and more positive outlook on life; that in turn will lead to positive speech and positive actions all of which will produce good or positive effects or "karma". But positive thinking by itself isn't enough. It won't work unless we unload some of our baggage and clutter. And that's what we'll start to do in the next chapter.

2

Releasing ourselves through forgiveness

What is forgiveness?

Forgiveness is all about letting go. It can be in the context of a person in authority granting a pardon for a wrong that has been committed or it may be that a person releases a wrongdoer from any debt or recompense. Both of these imply some sort of letting go. But in the more everyday sense, and of greatest relevance in our quest for finding the source of happiness within us, is the letting go of any anger or resentment we have, for whatever reason it has arisen.

When we think of forgiveness, we might think that we are doing someone else a big favour because we are releasing them from whatever negativity we might be holding against them – a grudge, anger or irritation or even simply a sense of blame. But that's just the ego making us feel a little bit grand. Let's be perfectly clear about this: the person who is released most of all is the one who forgives.

Why forgiveness is necessary for our happiness and well-being

If the one who forgives is the main beneficiary, then we can afford to be pretty generous with our forgiving! We'll be looking at this new-found beneficence from three angles: forgiveness towards ourselves, forgiving those who have harmed or offended us and cultivating a general attitude of forgiveness towards the world at large. That sounds a fairly tall order but it is possible in time. The important thing is to work towards it because the more we are able to forgive, the happier we will be and better human beings we will become. Forgiveness is necessary for our own development and isn't an option. Let's look at why.

Rather like an onion with its many layers, there is far more to a human being than the façade of the physical body. There are deeper layers. If we "peeled back" the physical layer, we would find something like a blueprint of what we see on the outside. This is sometimes called the etheric or vital body and the various meridians and other channels through which chi flows help to form this. If the etheric body goes out of balance, sickness arises in the physical body; if the etheric body is well-balanced, good physical health and well-being are the result. A little deeper than this is the subtle body through which feelings are experienced, sometimes called the emotional body, and deeper still is the mental body in which thoughts and imagination have their place. Each of these bodies is inter-linked with the others. For example, a negative thought will cause a reaction in the emotional body, so a bad feeling will arise; this in turn affects the balance of energy in the etheric body so our vitality and sense of well-being take a knock. This, if prolonged, can result in sickness or some other manifestation of poor health.

If we hang onto grievances, or thoughts of guilt in relation to ourselves, knots, stagnation and blocks in the flow of energy will arise in our mental body. These will have an effect on our emotions and these in turn will adversely affect the energy flow within the etheric body. Our vitality will go down and we just won't feel good. If we could see the aura of someone holding resentment, we would see dark patches in it, like black holes, with red flashes when the resentment is aroused. That doesn't make for a pretty sight and even if the aura cannot be seen by most people, it can be sensed. Resentment and anger are very ugly things. A number of things can happen if we hold onto past wrongs, whether they are our own mistakes or someone else's:

- *We will experience a lack of clarity* and our thinking will be distorted. Uncomfortable feelings or emotions, upset energy, a weakening of the immune system and generally feeling out of balance are inevitable. If we hold onto this for a long time, illness is very possible.

- *The subtle energy centre of the heart*, where warm feelings would normally arise, will be closed off – slightly when the memory of the resentment is dormant and greatly, or even completely, when the memory surfaces.

- *The body's circulation will be affected* by constrictions in the etheric body, the nervous system will be agitated and the endocrine system will be adversely affected.

It's not hard to see that negative thinking will eventually wear the body out as well as make the individual very unhappy.

Letting go of wrongs (or what are perceived as wrongs) is very good for our health and our happiness. On a wider level, society, too, needs to let go of many wrongs. Holding onto the past is resulting all over the world in warfare, famine and racism, to name but three. But society cannot let go unless the individuals who make up society let go in their own lives. So the responsibility for letting go goes beyond what is good for the individual.

Forgiving ourselves

Please ask yourself this question: "Is it selfish to forgive myself?" It seems OK to forgive others but self-forgiveness? To answer the question honestly, we have to distinguish between forgiving ourselves in the sense of letting go of guilty feelings and making excuses for harmful words or behaviour so we can do the same again. To forgive ourselves doesn't mean not to have a conscience; it means letting go of harmful feelings of guilt. Responsible or ethical speech and conduct (and, indeed, thinking) are vital aspects of the path of self-development so irresponsible attitudes are not being advocated here.

The essential point is that if we cannot let go of guilt within ourselves, we cannot forgive others truly and completely. If we can resent something within our own make-up, there are going to be things we will resent in others. So the short answer is that it is not selfish to forgive ourselves or, to put it another way, to have a sense of self-acceptance, quite the opposite.

Before we can let go, though, we need to know what it is we are holding onto. That isn't always easy but to try to undertake some sort of amateur self-analysis can be counter-productive – we can get hooked into all sorts of things – so sometimes it's helpful to sneak up on ourselves from another direction. Most people are not aware at a surface level that they hold anything against themselves and perhaps you responded to the question "Is it to selfish to forgive myself?" with "Forgive myself for what?" But ask people about their self-esteem and we normally get quite a different story. Most people are self-deprecating to some degree. To become happy people, we have to let go of those things that negatively affect our self-esteem. Poor self-esteem involves a sense of fear – fear of ourselves. Crazy, isn't it? But who would argue that the human race is anything but crazy?

So our starting point is to build up our self esteem. We don't need to analyse where we think we are failing because that's focusing on the negative. We simply start by building up a positive picture.

What follows in a moment is a powerful exercise for building up self-esteem. Don't underestimate it – it works. Find a place to sit quietly on your own and allow yourself a comfortable five minutes or a little longer if you wish:

Self-forgiveness by building up self-esteem

- *Visualise yourself seated in a totally empty room. Say to yourself, "I am." This is a positive statement. Repeat it a few times: "I am."*

- *Imagine someone coming into the room and placing some flowers at your feet. Hear this person say, "These flowers are for you because you are who you are."*

- *Embrace this other person. It is yourself: it is your soul, your spirit, your higher, wise self.*

- *See someone else come into the room. This person places a golden chalice at your feet and says, "This chalice is for you. It holds all opportunities in life and is always full."*

- *Pick up the chalice and embrace it. It is the sum total of all past and future actions.*

- *Feel yourself smiling inside and say to yourself, "I welcome all that comes because I am." As you do this, see yourself fill with light and be at ease.*

This technique should preferably be done once a day for a week and then whenever there is a feeling of self-doubt. By embracing our whole self and our past and future actions, we forgive everything about ourselves. In other words we *accept* who we are. In energy terms, this can have a very profound effect.

Sometimes, though, there can be something that really bothers us. In spite of doing the above exercise, or perhaps preventing us from doing it, memory of some specific mistake grinds into our conscience with a nagging sense of guilt. If there is a strong reaction like that, or if we are aware we are suppressing something, then we need to do something. Leaving it is just like the proverbial ostrich with its head buried in the sand. So what can we do? If we have harmed somebody, spoken out of turn, acted unjustly, omitted to do something or whatever it happens to be, we should use any opportunity we can to apologise or to put things right. If that is not possible or if no-one else is involved, we can use the following method:

Self-forgiveness for a specific action etc.

- *Visualise the person (or group) you have harmed or wronged, or if no-one else is involved, you should visualise your guide, teacher or other higher being for whom you have respect and loyalty. Simply explain yourself truly and honestly to this person (or group) and say, "I am truly sorry."*

- *Then see yourself attempting to put things right and making amends by bringing the action back to yourself or "undoing" the action.*

This method is very simple but its effect can be very deep indeed. Sometimes it may need to be done more than once. It all depends to what extent the sense of guilt has been ingrained but it is better to do it once and see how our feelings are affected over a period of time than to keep repeating it. Many of these techniques are like taking a medicine – it is important to allow time for healing to take place before taking another dose.

Forgiving those who have harmed or offended us

Firstly, we must understand very clearly that holding onto a grudge or resentment does not harm or hinder the other person involved. It may make things difficult or a little unpleasant but it really has no effect on the other person most of the time. Conversely, it is causing us great damage. It is also reducing our capacity to love others and to be a useful member of society.

Is there any reason why should we not forgive? The short answer is "no". There might be a million and one reasons why a finger can be pointed at someone who has done dreadful things but forgiveness does not involve condoning (in the sense of sanctioning or approving) wrong actions. So forgiveness is not about saying a terrible deed or omission is OK. Please let us be clear about this. Wrong actions are not to be condoned. It may be that on closer analysis of something, behaviour can be explained or understood better but that is not the same as condonation.

The essence of forgiveness is to release ourselves and free our own energy by seeing the truth that underlies the appearance. We need to see the deeper picture. Our resentment arises from false perception – we build up a picture of presumptions and judgments. We need to change our perception, and if we do the resentment dissolves.

There are many ways of doing this – for example by analysing all the causes and conditions that gave rise to the action we resent, by taking into account the law of karma and understanding some of its effects. But we don't normally have the time to do this, or the inclination. For very deep issues this may be necessary but there is a simpler method that is very practical and easy to use:

Forgiving others

- *See the other person as a child.*

24

It really is that simple. If we see the other person as a child, we will see that it is possible, inevitable even, for that person to make mistakes and even do serious wrongs. But a child is not judged or condemned for ever and eventually grows up and out of his or her bad habits. Each one of us is a child in spiritual terms. We are all thoroughly immature. So we need to understand when seeing the other person as a child that we are a child also and from time to time also make mistakes. Please don't underestimate this – it is incredibly effective and, in terms of releasing our energy, can be extremely profound.

Sometimes, however, someone may have hurt us very badly in the past and the wound is too deep for this method to work. In those circumstances we may need to meditate or think on the causes. If we do that, it is important that we have some guidance from someone who is skilled in these things; otherwise there is a danger of entrenching our hurt and resentment more deeply.

Cultivating an attitude of forgiveness

Forgiving ourselves and others for harm they have done us (or we perceive they have done us) is only part of the story. In one sense, those things are easier to work with because there is a specific point of focus – ourselves in building up self-esteem or seeing a person as if they were a child. But why do we get into the mess caused by resentment in the first place?

If we want to be happy and have a good sense of wellbeing, it is important that resentment isn't allowed to build up. If we let it, it is like accumulating a toxic substance in the body. If poison arises in the mind, there is a knock-on effect in the body. In the short-term, we feel pretty bad and in the longer term all sorts of maladies can arise in the physical body. So how can we avoid this self-poisoning process?

Human beings are very good at "pointing the finger" at other people. What experts we are at noticing the faults of other people! If we didn't thrive on it so much, the newspaper industry and half the social conversations in our communities would founder. That's the trouble.

Lack of forgiveness, or rather the establishing of blame or fault and holding onto that, arises from judgment or discrimination. Judgment comes from the basic sense of "I" that we talked about in the first chapter. There's "me" and there's "you and everyone else". We can call that a sense of separation – the opposite of unity – and the stronger the sense of separation, or "I" or ego, the stronger the tendency to judge and to blame. That in turn leads to a difficulty in forgiving or letting go and it becomes a vicious circle. The more we blame, the more the ego is inflated and the more judgmental we become.

It might sound a tall order, but to release ourselves fully it is necessary to develop an attitude of blamelessness. This is not to ignore the fact that dreadful things happen in the world, of course they do; but we don't know all the causes for everything because we can only ever see part of the picture. Rather than condemn the perpetrators it is better to recognise that certain actions lead to suffering.

So how can we live a life where we do not blame or judge? It is difficult because we must still be able to discriminate between what is harmful and what is good. Perhaps one of the most effective ways is to see that the world is a place of learning and experience and that *all* human beings are here to learn and must go through this learning process. If we can accept that, then we need to have the humility to recognise that there must be lessons for us to learn, otherwise we wouldn't be here; and if that is the case, we should concentrate on what we need to learn and not think that we can teach others or that we know better than them.

Here is a method that can be very helpful in developing an attitude of blamelessness when we see things going wrong:

Developing an attitude of "no blame"

- *First, watch how we think by asking ourselves these questions: "Am I judging?" "Am I casting blame?" This can be very revealing. Or: "Am I accepting things how they are for what they are or am I judging things as good or bad?"*

- *Second, release what is happening by saying, "I have not yet learnt all my lessons. All I see is someone trying to learn theirs. I pray that we all may learn our lessons and be free."*

- *Third, reinforce the idea of no blame by saying, "I release all humanity. There is no blame. We are all children striving to learn and grow up."*

The third point is good to do daily as well as when things crop up.

"There but for the grace of God go I" is a wonderful aphorism. If we were born with the same mental conditioning, parents, up-bringing, social conditions, body and nervous system as another person then, subject to the same circumstances and conditions, we would behave as they do.

To conclude this chapter on releasing ourselves through forgiveness, here is a meditation that is good to do periodically and can be very strengthening in our practice of "letting go".

A meditation on forgiveness

- *See yourself surrounded in light.*
- *See the rest of humanity surrounded in light.*
- *See the world surrounded in light.*

27

- *See shadows playing on the surface of the world: these are the shadows of what we call "wrongdoing". They are but temporary fluctuations and the light always resumes.*
- *See shadows and colours playing in humanity. These also are temporary and the light will resume.*
- *See shadows casting across yourself briefly. These are the shadows and fluctuations caused by your own thoughts and emotions but again, the light resumes.*
- *There is no blame, no fault, just the play of light.*

3

Why true generosity brings joy

The secret energy of the heart

Throughout the body there are a number of energy centres and in the area of the heart there is a very special one. At the physical level, energy radiates throughout the body from the heart through the cardiovascular system; at a more subtle level is the etheric or vital layer that underlies the physical body and within this there is a vital or etheric energy centre that corresponds to the physical heart. When there is imbalance in the vital or etheric body, sickness can arise. At a deeper level of our being is the emotional or feeling layer, sometimes called the emotional or astral body, and at a deeper level still is the mental body. Both of these subtle bodies have corresponding energy centres. Throughout all these layers, energy circulates and the heart centre in particular radiates energy throughout them. At the outer or physical level we know the good functioning of the heart is essential for good health but how much attention do we pay to the inner heart that governs the emotions and the way we think?

In the same way that the physical heart is concerned with supply, the emotional and mental heart centres, our feeling and thinking hearts, are also concerned with supply or giving. The more freely we can give of ourselves, the better the heart centres will function; similarly, the better they function, the more freely we can give. This means that the more open our mental or thinking heart is, the more the energy will circulate throughout the mental body – it will be healthier; the emotional heart centre will circulate more energy and be freer as will the etheric or vital energy, which affects our health. This is how the way we think can have an effect on our health and well-being. The energy of the heart is, therefore, particularly special and we should nurture it at all levels.

How joy can be cultivated through this energy

Our concern is with cultivating happiness and a concomitant of this is having a joyful heart. Joy is a deeper feeling of happiness, one that really springs from the heart and it arises when the inner heart centres start to open. If we do things that result in joy, it means that at an energy level the centres have started to change. These centres are said to be very much like flowers in the sense that they radiate from the middle outwards and can close or open rather like the petals of a flower. So joy arises when the energy in the inner heart begins to radiate or, to put it more poetically, as the petals of the heart flower start to open. Sometimes this flower is described as a lotus in bud which gradually opens as we become more loving and compassionate in nature.

If we want to experience joy, or experience it more deeply, we have to allow or encourage openness of heart so that there is an outward movement of energy. From time to time, events in life will cause, or rather trigger responses in us that cause, that outward flow of energy to retract, rather like the shadow from a cloud passing across the face of the sun can cause some types of flower to close their petals. This happens and will always happen – it's human life; the important thing is to live life in such a way that the general trend is for the heart to be increasingly more open – to be freer – so that life becomes increasingly joyful.

The positive effect on well-being and health

The key to these energy changes is to work from the inside outwards. In other words, the more subtle the energy we work with, the greater the effects. Joyfulness and happiness are states of mind and because the mind and emotions affect the vital or etheric body that informs the physical body, there is a direct bearing on health and sense of well-being.

When joy and happiness are experienced, it is because the mind is in a more natural state, unclouded by negative conditioning. The perception of life and everything around us is different. The beauty of a flower, for example, can deeply affect us when the mind is clear; dewdrops in the morning sun can appear like diamonds iridescent with penetrating colours; or a simple act of kindness can change how we view someone. All manner of things can happen and when they do, there is a response in the heart centre. Joy, warmth and gladness can be felt here and that response triggers, at a physical level, biochemical reactions in the body and brain. A greater sense of well-being is experienced – we feel good, there is less stress and the immune system is stronger.

A heightened sense of awareness

So many people have told me over the years how, as they have felt increasingly better within themselves, their understanding, appreciation and awareness of life have improved significantly. This is not just a change in intellectual functioning but something else goes on. As the more subtle energies improve, the knock-on effect in the physical body is not just one of health and well-being. The level of chi or prana, the vital energy that governs health and the whole functioning of the body, is improved and that has a direct bearing on the nervous system. This isn't rocket science – if we are in a room full of stale air, for example, we will feel dull until we can revitalise ourselves with some fresh air and exercise; and as that dullness is overtaken by freshness, our senses become more alert.

Joyousness has a similar effect. As we become happier, not only does our energy improve but our sense faculties become sharper as well. Colours appear more vibrant; we will hear, perhaps, more subtle nuances of sound and our senses of taste and smell may pick up different flavours and fragrances. It is not uncommon for people to change their eating habits to different types of food as increasing sense appreciation and awareness unfold.

These are just examples but the important thing is that our awareness and our senses inform the mind, so a cycle of improvement takes place. The joyful heart heightens perception and heightened perception helps to create the conditions for happiness and joy. Life becomes fuller and richer. When increasing richness to life isn't present, it means that there are barriers and we'll have a look at the reasons for those now.

Recognising barriers to joy

Barriers to joy arise purely as a result of internal signals. If we have had a bad or fearful experience, some memory of that is always retained and when something triggers that memory, clouds cross our horizon. In energy terms, we close up. Our heart centre shrinks and becomes pinched. We become joyless. If we are strong, we might be able to masquerade a smile for the benefit of others but inside we know we are not smiling. Our perception of things becomes clouded or distorted and our responses are not what they should be.

What happens then? We usually compound our difficulties by jumping to the wrong conclusions, by saying things that are hurtful or entirely inappropriate (or not saying something when we should) and generally reacting wrongly. There may well be a stress response in the body producing a biochemical reaction so our sense of well-being drops and if the reaction continues, our immune system takes a knock, too. The result becomes at the least an unpleasant and joyless experience which adds to the unpleasant residue in our memory bank.

It is possible, though, with persistence and with time, to overcome the triggers. As a first step, we need to be aware when they have arisen. That may sound obvious but actually most of us most of the time go from one moment to the next with fluctuations in temperament. One moment we can be happy then we'll hear something, see something or just have some thoughts which cause our feelings to dip; but rarely do we intelligently look at why that dip took place. We might see it in others more than in ourselves – a shadow passes across the face. But if we can look at that dip with the light of the mind, so to speak, it should be quite revealing.

The dip comes because our perception is wrong. All sorts of emotions can arise but they all fall into one of three categories, or we could say they have their roots in them: attachment and desire (which arise from I want, I like etc.), aversion, hatred and dislike (from which anger and jealousy arise, for example) and, thirdly, ignorance as to our own nature (which deludes us into thinking we are separate from everything else in the universe and gives rise to the ego).

The intelligent way of looking at it is not to analyse the historical causes of the emotion by trying to figure out what it was in our past, some childhood incident perhaps, that has triggered the emotional response but *merely to identify the emotion that is present*. If we are hurt by a remark or by the way we have been treated, for example, we can say or think to ourselves, "A feeling of being hurt is present." Keep saying it to yourself and eventually the feeling will subside. The important thing is not to apportion blame or cause – that's the ego's trick – simply identify the feeling. With practice, we might find a realisation dawning: that the feeling of hurt actually arises from attachment or pride, or perhaps both. Again, we don't try to judge that; instead, we merely say to ourselves, "A feeling of pride is present," or whatever it happens to be. *The vital thing, though, is not to judge; we want to become the observer of the feelings so that they become weaker and lose their power over us, and not get wound into them.* Gradually, the strength of these afflictive emotions, as they are sometimes called, and the frequency of their arising will diminish.

Why generosity opens the heart and brings joy

The art of generosity is a very powerful and remarkable thing. It is extraordinarily effective in changing our thought patterns, our emotions and the energies within our vital body, which affects our health and well-being. But it is an art. The skill in this art is acquired; some of it was almost certainly present when we were small children but for most of us a great deal of it has been knocked out of us or overshadowed by daily living. Western society has many strengths but one of its major drawbacks is the acquisitive style of life that it encourages. Life conditions us to want things for ourselves and so the natural innocence that gives rise to spontaneous giving is often absent. But that trend can be reversed and when we start to develop the generous spirit within us, a state of joyousness naturally arises.

The acquisitive style of life, which encourages us to accumulate and hold onto things, gives us an energy pattern of "holding on". That holding on might be in relation to possessions or money or to circumstances or relationships but it can also be in relation to less tangible things such as our time, our love, our caring and so on. Holding on, or failing to give wholeheartedly, actually deprives us of something. It prevents us from contacting our own nature and so instead of bringing happiness, everything we hold onto dearly brings a degree of stagnation into our energy system plus, of course, the fear of losing it.

Just for a moment, imagine holding something in your hand and someone is trying to take it from you. Notice how the tension in your hand increases as you tighten your grip. Conversely, if you want to give away whatever it is you are holding, notice the relaxation that comes. And did you notice that the tension wasn't just in the hand? It is impossible to grip the hand without causing tension up the whole arm. Mentally it is not much different. The sense of anxiety that can build up when we fear losing something causes a tension that runs right through us. It is no coincidence that the words "miserliness" and "miserable" come from the same Latin root meaning "wretched".

Now, when we give something, we have the opportunity to release mental and emotional tension. If we give easily, our energy will feel lighter because our heart centre will be freer. We just let go of whatever it is we have and, if we do it with loving kindness, we give it a little helpful push on the way. We then have more energy; we feel better. It might seem odd but the more we give, the better off we are.

But we have to give *well*. By that, I mean if we give begrudgingly or with reservation, we hold something back. There will be some benefit but not as much. If we hold back when we give, it is like letting something go out of our hand but there is till some tension in our grip. Similarly, if we give something with expectation of recognition or of thanks, there is a little tension in that giving; we are not giving wholeheartedly because we have added a condition to it – there is a subtle acquisitiveness to our giving and so it isn't selfless.

That is why generosity is an art. We have to re-educate ourselves into becoming totally generous human beings. We need to learn to give unconditionally and, as we learn to do so, our happiness will increase because the "petals of the heart lotus" will be opening, letting in the sunshine of our true nature. But it does take some training for most of us, for if we are honest, we might be good at giving some things but certainly not at giving others.

There is a lovely story of a businessman approaching the Buddha for advice. The businessman said that he understood much of what the Buddha was teaching about becoming a better human being but felt he was unable to do so because of his own avarice. On his own admission, he was extremely mean and couldn't let go of anything. The Buddha had the man put something into his left hand and then practise giving it to the right hand. Silly though this might sound to us, it was the first time the man had practised giving in any way at all. That was how it started and, because he was determined to overcome his own miserliness, he gradually expanded the practice until he was able to give small things to members of his family and later became a most generous man indeed.

We may not be in that category but it can certainly be helpful to practise some mental exercises that help to increase the flow of energy in us through visualising generosity. This following one is an excellent start. I suggest you try doing it for 3 or 4 minutes to start with (longer if you feel like it) and then do it 2 or 3 times a day for a week – perhaps on waking and on going to bed plus once during the day if you find time. Even doing it for a couple of minutes is a good boost.

First technique for generating joy

This is based on one of the major causes of joyfulness – an open heart. An open heart is based on selflessness and giving. We should normally start in a small way:

- *Start by visualising yourself giving – as you do now. Just see instances when you give, whether that be material or of time or energy or giving of yourself. Then gradually increase that – seeing yourself give more and more. Build up the picture of giving.*

- *There is no need to fear because there is an endless pot we are giving from in this exercise. Give all sorts of things – smiles, material things, money, water to the thirsty, healing and so on. Have no limit on the imagination: just give, give, give and be happy in that giving.*

How to sow seeds to create joyfulness

In chapter 1 we took a brief look at the law of cause and effect and how every effect, i.e. every set of circumstances, has its causes. Things don't happen just by chance even when they appear that way – there *must* be causes, whether we understand them or not. That means that if we want to create an effect, in our case the effect of being joyful, we must create the necessary causes for that to happen.

Here's a little experiment you might like to try:

- *Take a few moments now to recall a time when you were happy and experienced joy. Recollect the feeling that arose and stay with that feeling. Now think – why did that feeling arise at that time in the past? And why did it arise just now?*

You should have been able to identify some of the causes that led to those feelings or at least have appreciated that there were causes. Appreciation of others and of what we have, appreciating beauty, giving selflessly, being given a lovely smile – these are the sort of things that can give rise to joyful moments in everyday life, and they occur because there is a sufficient degree of positivity in our mental make-up. In other words, joyfulness will be experienced to the degree that the mind has positive seeds sown in it.

To create the experience of joy and happiness more, we need to create more positive seeds than negative ones. Eventually we should aim to sow no negative seeds at all but we are human and it is inevitable that we will think, speak and behave less than perfectly for some time to come! But the more positive seeds we sow, the less effect the negative ones will have. So what are these seeds? *Each time we are selfless, we create a positive seed and each time we are selfish, we create a negative one.* If, for example, we give to a charity collector in the street simply out of kindness or compassion, that will give rise to a positive effect. There will be a tickle of joy in the heart. But if we give to avoid being pestered or because we don't want to feel guilty, or even so that we look better in the eyes of others, that act of giving does not carry the same positive effect. The giving might be the same, outwardly at least, but the attitude at the time determines whether it has a positive, neutral or negative effect.

Although joy is experienced as a feeling, it arises in the mind and so that is where the greatest potential is for sowing seeds or causes that will result in joy. The technique of *giving with the mind* is a very powerful one and this following exercise is wonderful for increasing a sense of abundance in us:

Visualisation for abundance

- *Sit comfortably and totally relaxed. Create an image in your mind of being very rich. You are a controller of great wealth, of abundance of all sorts.*

- *Now visualise passing all that wealth onto others and, at the same time, others still are passing great abundance to you. Feel, if you can, a great circulation of energy which is passing freely to you and from you. Wonderful!*

This is what life is like – a great circulation of energy. If we circulate physical resources, we will gain physical wealth and enjoy physical abundance. If we circulate joyous resources, we will gain joy, joyous abundance. Whatever we circulate, we gain. This is a natural law.

Moving towards an attitude of selflessness

Selflessness and generosity are, in essence, the same thing but for them to make a huge difference in our lives – and they will – there has to be a change in our outlook. It is not a question of doing the odd kind act here and there; we have to move towards a state of mind where our attitude towards life is one of generosity. In other words we need to work towards developing a state of consciousness where we are naturally and spontaneously generous-hearted. That doesn't mean we become a "soft touch", giving in to every request – that arises when we allow ourselves to be led by our emotions without having the balance of wisdom – but it does mean dissolving the residual hardness that most of us carry in our hearts from the knocks and pains of life.

Generosity and selflessness are really a matter of simply letting go and that implies that the barriers to developing an attitude of selflessness are the things we hold onto. We have to overcome those barriers because they are the things that are preventing our natural state of joyousness from arising; so the task we need to undertake is to identify those things we hang onto – our "attachments", as they are sometimes called.

Here is a very useful exercise that helps us to identify our attachments and to begin to let go of them. I say "begin to let go" because attachments, by their very nature, arise from a habit of thinking and habits have to be undone; but by identifying them, and having the desire to do something about them, we take a major step in their demolition! The exercise is in three parts and it is better to do the three parts one straight after the other so allow yourself 10 to 15 minutes to do it all if you can.

1. Identifying attachments

- *Sit quietly where you won't be disturbed. Looking at your life, what are the things you cannot do without or think you cannot do without? (Ignore basic life essentials for the purpose of this exercise.) Take a good 5 minutes – and be honest with yourself!*

2.   Recognising the burden

- *Jot down on a piece of paper the attachments you have just identified.*
- *Which of those things you have noted are a burden to you? The burden is not necessarily the thing itself but your attitude towards it.*
- *Realise that where we perceive a burden, there is a barrier to joy.*

3.   Releasing our attachments

- *Sit quietly again, perhaps with eyes closed, and visualise giving away all those things you are attached to and the mental attachment that hold you to them. Visualise actually giving them to another person – either someone you love or an imaginary person, more than one person if you wish. (You are not making the other person attached, just releasing the attachment.)*

What we are doing in a small way is starting to neutralise the attachments in our mind. Attachments are negative in terms of energy and by "giving them away" we are charging them with positive energy which helps to neutralise them. In our daily life we should continue to do this to maintain the momentum of the process we have just started. We can do it in a number of ways – mentally offering our attachments, whether that be to our spiritual roots, to friends, neighbours or someone close to us, whichever we feel comfortable with. And do it with the intention of benefiting the other person, of making them happy. This works because we are mentally giving up what we cling to most. (Don't tell the other person what you are doing. They are not actually involved at all. This is personal to you and, as with many practices, it will undermine the effect if you start trying to explain it to others.)

A simple technique for releasing our generous spirit

Having started to address the barriers, we are ready to start developing the attitude of selfless generosity. This technique is incredibly effective at releasing energy:

- *Say quietly (i.e. mentally) to everyone you meet:*
- *"I give you all that I have. I wish you great joy and a happy, long life."*

The exact words are not crucial but the thought must be sincere. Really mean what you say. "I give you all that I have" is a great releasing of any attachment we may have. "I wish you great joy and a happy, long life" is wishing the very best for the other person and by wishing happiness for others we sow very positive seeds indeed for our own and others' peace of mind and happiness.

- *"I give you all that I have. I wish you great joy and a happy long life."*

Please practise this often and always with sincerity. If you do nothing else from this book, please do this because it really will bring great rewards. If you see someone suffering, use the same or similar words and add:

- *"I wish you release from all your suffering."*

So, if they are sick, wish them health. If they are worried, wish them freedom from worry, and so on. Whatever unhappy state or condition they have, wish them the opposite. We don't say the words out loud but think them as though we were saying them.

Practise this wonderfully simple but effective technique on others as much as you can, whether you know them or not. The effect on our mind and energy system is quite remarkable. And don't forget yourself in this – we often think we don't deserve happiness, so imagine practising it to an image of yourself, too. That odd person we see in the bathroom mirror deserves happiness, so wish it for them!

Dealing with obstacles to being generous

No matter how well-intentioned we are, sometimes the brakes will go on and we will have all sorts of doubts about whether we should give or not. We may even recoil at the thought of giving. A common example that people often give is that they feel uncomfortable about giving to someone begging because they don't know whether the person is genuinely needy or is carrying out a deception. The mind is an odd thing; it creates all sorts of reasons not to give. There are many charitable organisations carrying out hugely deserving work but does the mind say, "They spend too much on administration so don't deserve my money"? All this sort of reasoning may be correct – some of the time. In some countries, begging is an absolute necessity for some people whilst in others it can be a lucrative way of life and is nothing but a deception on the gullible. How do we know what to do?

The thing we need to do is to act in such a way that our heart remains open. True generosity is spontaneous – it isn't a question of logical reasoning. Our heart should remain open so that our outlook on life is a joyful one. If we feel a pinch in the heart, a withdrawal of energy or a have a closing feeling when we are asked for something it means that we aren't dealing with the situation in the best way. If we are not sure whether to give or not, or are not happy to give, or perhaps can't afford to give, we can still give from the heart by giving a silent blessing. Inwardly, we simply wish the other person the best possible circumstances. This ensures that we don't close up inside and we are still giving something – the best we can possibly think of.

Why counting our blessings frees up energy

"Count your blessings" is such a wonderful piece of advice. When we think positively, our energy increases and, conversely, when we think negatively our energy takes a down-turn. "Counting our blessings" means to take stock of all the positive things in our lives. For many people, that's foreign language because all they see is what they haven't got. But if we look at what we have in a positive way, we are fuelling our energy system with positive fuel.

Positive thoughts create lighter energy patterns in mental matter – our "mental body" – which in turn cause positive effects in our emotional body. Our vital or etheric body – that part of our system which carries chi or vital energy – becomes "positively charged" and this directly affects our health and sense of well-being. More than that, counting blessings – acknowledging the good aspects of life – starves the negative thought processes.

As we acknowledge what we have, a sense of appreciation and gratitude is cultivated. We realise that, whatever our material status or our health, we are actually very rich. And as we realise how rich we are inside, we know we have a limitless reservoir from which to give and that is the true root of generosity.

4

The amazing energy of love

What is true love?

If we want to be happy, we have to be able to love. That doesn't mean we have to have a personal relationship because there are many people who live very happily on their own, but it is necessary to express love in one way or another. That begs the question, "What is love?" Is it a feeling, an energy, an emotion or a mental attitude? Or perhaps it is all these things? Do we know when we are experiencing true love as opposed to other feelings or emotions? Do we kid ourselves that we love something or somebody when there is some other process going on? How many people, often young but not necessarily so, fall "hopelessly in love" to discover later that that "love" was merely infatuation?

We have all experienced giving and receiving love and have also felt, or imagined we have felt, its absence. Love is always pure – that is its nature – but the experience we have of it as human beings, with all our conditioning and idiosyncrasies, is often so heavily disguised or covered with all manner of emotions and thought processes that its purity is often hidden. Love can only truly be experienced in innocence, when our outlook is unmarred by expectations, by fears or by selfish desires. We will be looking in this chapter at how amazingly transforming love is and what magic it can and will weave into our lives if we will let it. To do that, we have to start to have an understanding of what love is and what it isn't.

Why all love is unconditional and why attachment hurts

Many people talk about "unconditional love" as though it were some special, spiritual, new-age thing that has to be distinguished from a poor relation called "conditional love". Visions come to mind of pure souls sitting atop mountains in cross-legged postures with beaming smiles radiating "unconditional love" for the benefit of the world, pausing from time to time, no doubt, to sip pure water or perhaps some green tea. Some talk about "unconditional love" with as much dispassion and dryness as a dehydrated tea-leaf. Love needs fire, it needs heat and it needs the fluidity of water and the reality of earth, otherwise it isn't real. There is no such thing as "conditional love" because love is pure. If there is love, there is love, full-stop. Someone said to me once, "I love everybody, all humanity, unconditionally." Had that been true, she would have been filled with a passion so great that she would not have been able to rest until every last drop of suffering was removed from the world. Anyone coming near her would have felt the greatest warmth from her, as we can from anyone who is filled with love; unfortunately, it was just a bland statement which at best meant she didn't actually dislike anybody.

What can mar the expression of love and is sometimes mistaken for love is *attachment*. Attachment is when we hold onto something because we want to keep it. If it is taken away from us, we feel loss and if we think we might lose it, we feel threatened or insecure. This can happen with regard to material things, to our health, to our lifestyle – in fact, if you can think of it there can be attachment to it. As a general rule, though, we don't mistake attachment to those things as love. With relationships, it is not so easy to distinguish between attachment and love. Do we become attached to people? Of course we do, because we know that when many sorts of relationship end, people feel loss, grieving, anger and so on. But it isn't love, that gives rise to these difficult, and very human, reactions and emotions.

Suppose, for example, that a young woman – let's call her Jill – falls in love with Ben. They start a relationship and Ben tells Jill that he loves her very much. They soon decide to live together and at first everything seems to be going well. Then one day, Jill sees Ben flirting with her best friend in a way that suggests to her something might be going on between them. Later Jill challenges Ben; they argue and become angry with each other. That's a very simplistic outline of a fairly common type of situation but the question is, to quote the title of a famous Tina Turner song, "What's love got to do with it?"

When we start a relationship with someone, it is because there is an attraction. There is something in that other person we are attracted to, something that we like and don't want to be without. "Isn't that love?" one might say and the answer is, "No, it isn't." Love may arise, and often does, but the desire for the other person is attachment. That isn't meant to sound mercenary but the truth is, when we start a relationship, or have the desire to start a relationship with someone, it is because we see something in the other person that will help to make us feel more complete. It is a natural thing that we seek things in life to make us feel "whole", more fulfilled; but that in itself isn't love. What we are doing is seeking something for ourselves. Sounds harsh, doesn't it? But it's true. This is attachment and the result of attachment is that when the object of our attachment is threatened, or rather our relationship with it is threatened, we feel pain.

Love, on the other hand, is nothing so volatile or unstable. Love is totally selfless. To love means we don't seek anything for ourselves; if we love someone, we want them to be happy for their own sake – not because seeing them happy makes us feel better. Most personal relationships will have an element of attachment in them but the important thing is that there must be the selfless aspect also. It has been said that "ideal relationships are based on giving" and we must be able to receive well, too. And love doesn't just occur in personal relationships; we all develop love for all manner of people, and many for animals and nature. It is possible and natural, for example, to love those we work with or meet with. The point is, love does not involve desire for the other person nor sentimental attachment, or at least if it is there, we should be able to distinguish between desire and attachment on the one hand and "true" love on the other.

The purpose of us spending a little time differentiating between love and attachment is not to condemn attachment but rather to emphasise the difference. We can then guard against strengthening attachment, with the inevitable pain that will someday cause as the object of our attachment changes or is lost, and instead build up the selfless aspect, love, which will reduce pain and bring about lasting happiness.

Understanding love as energy

Love is a very real energy. Everything in the universe is energy and love is part of it. If love weren't energy, it wouldn't affect anything but we know from our experience that it does; it changes things. We know if we love, we feel different, our body feels different, our vitality changes and life is better. People who live on their own and have a pet to care for, for example, tend to be healthier and live longer than those who live on their own with no outlet for love. So love does something.

Some of the ancient wisdom teachings speak of love as being the unifying energy of the universe. It holds things together and provides cohesiveness. We can see in families and other groups that where there is selfless caring those groups hold together very strongly. Those who have the gift of being able to see energies and auras describe the beautiful colours that emanate from people when they express love. Simply, we radiate energy of a very special kind when we love.

If we think, then, of love in terms of energy rather than simply as a feeling, we can begin to understand that it is a hugely transforming agent. It transforms us and, on an energy level, it can affect others. One of those effects is to heal, which we shall look at now.

Love as a healing agent

When we love, we send forth a great wave of positive energy and, because of its tendency to bring about cohesiveness, it heals. Love will heal rifts in relationships of all kinds, we know that; but it can also help to bring about healing of the body and emotions. A person who loves will tend to heal more quickly than someone who is very negative; they will also tend to fall ill less often because the immune system is stronger. This is partly because the happier we are, the more endorphins ("happy biochemicals") the body produces. There is also another aspect: the person who loves has less tension and restriction in the body with the result that both blood and chi (the vital energy of the body) flow more easily. So, quite unwittingly, the lover automatically nourishes his or her own body. This provides conditions in which the body will heal more easily. Negative emotions, those feelings that rise up and cause us pain, will arise less often because the positive energy of love will tend to neutralise or at least lessen the impact of them and so, over a period of time, the emotional body becomes healthier too.

By loving, we don't just heal ourselves, though. Love creates a positive energy field around us that affects other people. Unless the other person blocks us off by putting up mental barriers, our positive energy will bring about some effect in their energy field. It may only be a very small effect and perhaps just a fleeting one but some change there will be. If the other person is very negative, the effect will probably be negligible but even so, there are many who recount instances where an apparently negative person has been less so when loving or healing thoughts have been directed towards them. Imagine, then, the effect if the other person is receptive: they will receive a good boost of energy and healing processes will be enhanced by that.

Really successful healers are not those who just "lay on hands", although that can be an effective method in certain circumstances; no, the really successful healers are those who love, irrespective of who the other person is. Those in the medical and healing professions who truly love their work and love and care for their patients achieve far more than those who don't but we don't have to be a healer in the traditional sense or in one of the caring professions in order to heal. If we are human and love, we heal because that is one of the amazing effects of the energy of love.

The purifying effect of love

Love is a great purifier. There is much enthusiasm about detoxifying the body and bookshops abound with titles on the subject. Supermarkets, even, having shelves full of food containing diabolical amounts of rubbish now make a play on selling products that will help to detoxify the system. "So-and-so's marvellous 7, 14 or 28 day detox plan will make you feel so much younger, vital, radiant etc. etc." Great stuff; no doubt these plans, diets and so forth work well and it has been proved beyond any doubt that filling the body with toxins and junk food makes us feel pretty awful. But life isn't ruled by the body and we are not just a body, so if we are going to detoxify ourselves, wouldn't it be good to find something that detoxifies the mind and emotions as well? After all, it is the mind and emotions that govern our thinking, our speech and our behaviour and behaviour includes the act of putting food into our bodies. If we can look after the mind and emotions, the body will follow suit. It never ceases to amaze me that we humans are quite happy to spend time in the bathroom in the morning so that our bodies don't offend but very few people are prepared to spend a few minutes spiritually preparing the mind for the day ahead. Some spiritual teachers with considerable insight have said that if we could see the polluting effects of our minds and emotions on the world, we would be shocked to see how devastating they are – far worse than what we normally term pollution.

Love purifies because it uplifts our mind; the "rate of vibration" of the mind is raised or in other words it becomes lighter. As the mind becomes lighter, so do the emotions and our vitality – we are happier and have more energy; we know this from experience. As these aspects become lighter, the dross or impurities start to get thrown off. Imagine a plate or a turntable that is spinning slowly. Objects on it stay where they are purely from their inertia; their own weight keeps them where they are. Now imagine the spinning action speeding up. The objects start to move towards the edge and the faster the rate of spin, the closer to the edge they go and eventually they are thrown off. Something similar happens to our system. Negative thinking and negative emotions start to get thrown off by the lighter, positive energy that starts to flow through our system as we love more and become happier. This effect on mental, emotional and vital levels of our being also carries through to the physical level and those who have a deep love for all around them build up fewer toxins from the environment because the body throws them off far more readily.

So love is a great purifier. We don't go around trying to love in order to have a "grand detox", of course, but it is helpful to understand that love is hugely transforming and has only positive benefits. Sometimes we will find that our mood is less up-beat and that some of those negative thoughts will creep back in; that's normal and natural, but the more we love, the less often, and the less deeply, those things will come in. The important thing is to start the trend in the right direction. Life will still throw things at us from time to time but when it does, we will be able to handle them much more easily.

Why people are selective in what and whom they love

Love is not a deliberate act although, as we shall see a little later, it is possible to train the mind to enable us to love more easily. But although the capacity to love brings the capacity for happiness, for some reason we don't love everybody equally and it is indeed a rare human being who loves all others. When we express love for someone or something, the heart centre opens like a flower in the sun and that, as we saw earlier, gives us the experience of joy. If we were able to have that flower blossoming at all times, would it not be a marvellous thing? It would be an amazing experience because life would a total expression of love and joy. Long-term, that is an ideal aim but right now we will find that sometimes we feel loving, at other times we don't feel love at all and might even harbour negative feelings, whilst at still others, which may be the majority of the time if we are honest with ourselves, there is neither one nor the other, just neutrality or indifference.

Although we might be able to find innumerable detailed reasons as to why this is so, there is in essence one reason: we see others as separate from us and different in nature. When we love, it is because we recognise in the object of our love something akin to our own nature and when we don't love, we don't have that recognition; we see in the other something alien to us. Underneath the veneer of our personality – the complex of body, emotions and thoughts

– we all share the same spiritual nature and the purpose of life is to find that nature within. At times we *can* see it and when we recognise everyone else as exactly the same at the very root of their being, a resonance occurs that causes ripples of joy in the heart. So often, though, that recognition isn't there and that lack of recognition is the cause of all conflict, both inner and outer. Disputes arise from that lack of recognition, that incorrect view; dishonesty arises from it, anger arises from it and indifference has its source there, too. All negativity and all indifference stem from this wrong view that might be called separatism. If I give to you, I give to myself; if I take from you, I take from myself. If I love, I enrich myself; if I feel anger or hostility, I deprive myself. Such is the truth of recognising or failing to recognise the same nature or unity of all beings.

How this selectiveness affects our happiness and well-being

By failing to see that everyone shares the same nature, *is* the same nature, the heart centre oscillates; sometimes it is opening and at other times it closes. The effect of this is that the degree of happiness fluctuates. When the experience of love is present, our energy and vitality rise and when it is absent, they drop. When we love, we radiate something and our aura expands; when we don't, it recedes. This happens because love connects us to the universe; when we love, when we recognise and connect with others, we "plug in" to universal energy, so to speak. At other times, we disconnect ourselves and run on our own batteries, which have limited life and limited power.

By choosing not to love, and there is a certain amount of conscious choice in it, we restrict ourselves. We decline to engage fully with life. Painful experiences in the past may be the reason for some of that non-engagement but much of it arises from apathy and selfishness. Love is passionate, fiery and outgoing hence the radiance it brings. Opposite qualities turn inward and nourish the ego that we spoke of earlier. The radiance of love, on the other hand, nourishes all and in that nourishing increases our happiness and well-being. By not loving at times, we cut ourselves off from that. The question is, do we want to continue doing that when it is preventing our happiness from coming to fruition?

Some might argue that it's human nature to be selective in this way, and that would be quite right. But that doesn't mean we can't do anything about it. The contrary argument is that we *should* do something about it because what purpose is life unless it is to improve ourselves as human beings and to improve the world?

Expanding our capacity to love through selflessness

If we examine how much we love, we will probably find that we express love unwittingly and effortlessly much, or at least some, of the time, whether for people, animals, nature or anything else. But if we are honest with ourselves, we may also find that we do not love all people, all animals and all nature as much as we think we might. At best, we might acknowledge that we should and may even make a mood out of believing that we do, but that doesn't generate the energy of love that we have talked about. So how can we extend the expression of love to more people than we do, and how can we deepen and strengthen that love?

A clue lies in the expression of selflessness because, as we have seen, the extent to which we are selfish blocks the expression of love. But to be *totally* selfless is a tall order for most people and Rome wasn't built in a day! So we start off slowly and the best and easiest way is to start increasing our selflessness towards someone we love already.

An exercise in increasing love through selflessness (1)

- *Bring to mind someone you know and love. Visualise them clearly. Feel a warm glow in the heart as you visualise them.*

- *Now visualise giving everything you have, absolutely everything to them. Give it all with love, with a desire to please and to make them happy. Do this with genuine fondness and see the other person smiling with genuine happiness.*

When you first try this, you may find that you can only do it for a few seconds or that imagining giving everything away is difficult. You may find yourself objecting because giving everything away seems rather preposterous – "how would I live and what possible use would the other person have for all that?" – are the types of objection that might rise to the surface. If you can only manage a few seconds, just relax and try the exercise again later; it isn't designed to be a "one-off" but something to be built up, because what we are doing is freeing up our energy. If there are intellectual objections, just bring to mind that this isn't a vision of reality we are trying to conjure up; it is an exercise to help us release our attachment to things and to experience a sense of total selflessness towards another person.

Soon, though, if not straightaway, you will have a rather delightful feeling as the expression of love and the movement of energy through the heart centre bring a sense of joy, connectedness and total release. Try doing this exercise at various times over the next few days and perhaps try placing yourself on a scale of, say, 1 to 10 on how fully you feel you are expressing love during it. You might be pleasantly surprised at the progress.

How to deepen this love

No matter how much we already love, the above exercise will bring very positive results. Our capacity for love is immense and will continue to grow and deepen whether we start from a point of loving very little or from being very warm-hearted already. It is rather like a tender plant – if we nurture it, it will thrive. Once we are happy with the exercise and feel it is working for us, we can take it a stage further.

Our visualisation involved giving away everything that was ours and that helps to open the heart centre by releasing attachment and by giving. The desire for the other person's happiness is paramount and although we know that objects in themselves will not bring happiness, to be willing to give things away in order to bring about another person's happiness is the point. To deepen that effect, we can visualise giving not only everything that is ours but everything that our imagination is capable of visualising. This next exercise is a development of the last and we start off by doing as we did before:

An exercise in increasing love through selflessness (2)

- *As before, bring to mind someone you know and love. Visualise them clearly and feel a warm glow in the heart.*

- *Now visualise giving everything you have, absolutely everything to them. Give it all with love, with a desire to please and to make them happy. Do this with genuine fondness and see the other person smiling with genuine happiness.*

- *Now increase the flow of energy through the heart centre. Do this by increasing what is given: beautiful scenery, the stars, the sky and so on. Just continue giving, giving and giving. Eventually we give the whole universe, the whole cosmos, because there is nothing that we wouldn't give. And all the time, see the increasing happiness and delight of the other person. The whole thing should give the greatest delight. The happier they become, the happier we become!*

Remember that this is an exercise in self-development, so don't go round telling people that you have given them everything and are making them happy! They won't appreciate it and may well make some deprecatory comment that will totally deflate you and put you off practising. Also, don't look for signs of increasing happiness in the other – you are working on yourself, no-one else, in this. Having given that cautionary note, do please enjoy this. It contains the essence of offering, which is still strong in some cultures in the world but sadly has almost disappeared in our materialistic society.

How to increase our happiness by extending our love

If we can increase happiness by expressing love and generosity towards someone we love, what will happen if we start to generate the intention to do the same towards all people? The answer should be obvious: the heart energy centre will be open more often and will close less so our joyfulness will be more constant. Think about it – if you are with someone you are fond of, or perhaps are talking about them, your happiness factor is up, right? And if you are with someone you are not so keen on, what happens to it? It drops; the happiness factor is lower or perhaps not even there at all, your energy centres close a little and your radiant aura of energy is not so radiant. But what purpose does that serve? None. All it does is to reinforce the "not good" feeling that arises when we see that person. Some people feel they are meting out a deserved punishment to someone they don't like by withdrawing any feeling of goodwill but really they only punish themselves by thinking and acting in that way. Most of the time, though, feeling negative towards people isn't the problem; the problem is having a feeling of neutrality or indifference. In a way, that's worse for us because we don't even notice it. Our eyes are closed towards them and we walk around with blinkers on. Walk down any street and see how many people smile at you or even cast a glance your way; unless you live in a small community, there probably won't be many, if any. There is no friendliness because most people are terribly indifferent in our society today and indifference is a bigger hurdle than negativity, strange though that may seem.

Breaking the bonds of indifference

Our task, then, in increasing happiness is to use the energy of love to rid ourselves of indifference. This following exercise is a very good start in that direction. As in the last exercises, we use the power of the imagination. The imagination works because energy follows thought and the more clearly and enthusiastically we can build up a picture, the more the energy will flow.

Expanding the heart to overcome indifference

- *Visualise someone you don't know very well or someone you neither like nor dislike. You can also use an imaginary person at first, if you prefer.*
- *Generate a feeling of love towards this person. Try to feel a warm glow in your heart. Just like you, he or she is a person with feelings.*
- *Now visualise offering everything you have, absolutely everything, to this person. See yourself offering it all with love and with a desire to make the other person happy.*

- *Increase the flow of energy by seeing yourself offering everything in the universe to delight them more and more.*

- *Do this exercise with genuine fondness.*

You may have felt considerable warmth in your heart but if you didn't, don't worry. This exercise can be done again and again and gradually you will start feeling a greater sense of friendliness and a growing love for humanity. It's a childishly simple exercise to do but deceptively effective. Do please try it.

The question is often asked, "What about someone we actually feel badly about – someone we really feel negative towards? Can we use this exercise with them?" We can use it but it is more effective at overcoming neutral feelings and we don't want to reinforce inadvertently any negative feelings we may be harbouring. As we overcome indifference, we will normally find that negative emotions are weakened anyway so, for the time being at least, just use it in the way outlined.

The extraordinary effect of loving kindness and how to live it

Once we have experienced the rather pleasant effect of developing warmth instead of an indifferent or neutral feeling, it is a relatively easy and natural step to develop an attitude, or outlook on life, of loving kindness. Loving kindness is a state of mind where we actually cherish the existence, happiness and well-being of others. If we can cultivate that, our life will be rich and full no matter what our personal circumstances are. A life filled with loving kindness is one where our natural motivation and desire is to make the world a better place for everyone, even if what we do directly affects only one life, rather than seeing what we can get out of the world for ourselves, which is what our traditional education and upbringing largely prepares us for.

A person who is filled with loving kindness radiates a very special quality. Think of a person who has affected you at some time by their kindness towards you. Wasn't there something special coming from them? Perhaps at the time, or maybe later on, you felt some warmth or appreciation or even love towards them. Now imagine someone who felt that loving kindness towards everyone they came across and think of the effect they would be having on everything and everyone around them. There would be a tremendous aura about them, wouldn't there? It would touch and disarm almost everyone and they would have a warmth and smile that would melt hearts. If you have had the good fortune to be in the presence of such a person, you will know how utterly remarkable an effect there is. Now imagine yourself to be someone like that. What does it feel like? It might feel perfectly natural or it could feel a little strange at first but if you are able to imagine it, it means that such a state of being is possible to achieve. If it is too far a stretch for the imagination now, just try to imagine having that state of friendliness and kindness towards all those you come into contact with during your daily life.

By starting to think this way, life will start to change. Little by little, the natural kindness that is you will surface more and more. There will be occasions or even periods when it won't be there because challenges and painful memories will cause it to run for cover at times; but persist and enjoy being in that state of kindness as often as possible and the benefits will start to accumulate. They will accumulate for you because your happiness and your potential for happiness will grow very naturally and the "downtimes" will occur less frequently. Be careful not to let the ego interfere because ego and love are diametrically opposed; so if any sense of pride creeps in, loving kindness won't be there, whatever the appearance that is presented to others. So be genuinely kind, never smug, and allow that beautiful flower of your heart centre to blossom.

5

How to cultivate inner serenity

Why we naturally desire inner peace and tranquillity

Whenever I give introductory sessions on meditation to
groups, it is always a major surprise to them how relaxing
and calm they feel after only a few minutes of a very simple
meditative exercise. Many say they come because they
want to experience some calmness or tranquillity but they
never expect it to arise within themselves. As we live in a
society where virtually anything can be bought, perhaps we
are conditioned to think that tranquillity is the same. Of
course we can purchase the opportunity to go to peaceful
surroundings if we wish and we can buy relaxing music
and so forth to listen to. At great expense we could have
the experience of spending time in a flotation tank or
some other artificial environment. But we don't need to do
any of these things in order to experience inner serenity.
Perhaps those who come to the introductory sessions are
expecting me to give them something but all they get is the
opportunity to be with themselves. And that is the amazing
thing – peacefulness is not something separate from any of
us; it is us, it is our true nature.

Fulfilment can only come when we are peaceful inside because it is only when we are peaceful that we begin to be more in touch with who we really are – and that is the simple reason why each and every one of us, consciously or unconsciously, desires inner peace and tranquillity. It is natural to want it but it cannot be bought; it has to be discovered. A very busy person might say that they have far too much to do and that they thrive on stress and stimulus. Their whole system is in a more or less permanent state of excitation. If we are like that, we tend to seek more and more things and try to find fulfilment that way but we are not in touch with our true nature; in fact, we become blind to the possibility of its existence simply because the mind and body are so agitated that we think whatever it is we want from life is to be found "out there" rather than "in here". At some point, though, we will know that "out there" is not the answer and that we have to look within.

Understanding the relationship of mind and body

To understand how tranquillity is cultivated, we need to appreciate the special relationship of the mind and the body. Although in many respects the two are quite distinct, the mind is experienced and utilised through the vehicle of the brain and the nervous system, which are most definitely parts of the body; and we know only too well from our own experience that if the mind is agitated, there is a feeling of disturbance in the body. It is also difficult to maintain a calm mind if the body is upset. If the chemical balance of the body is upset through illness, wrong food or exposure to pathogens, for example, our thinking and our moods can be strongly affected. Conversely, it is also true that if the mind is calm, the biochemical balance is much better, the immune system is stronger and our energy is better.

Tests on meditators have shown the very close relationship of a calm mind to reactions in the body. Within minutes of starting to meditate, the breath rate slows down, the blood pressure drops and there is greater coherence in the electronic waves produced by the brain. People who take up t'ai chi ch'uan, using gentle, co-ordinated movements of the body, find a calming effect on the mind and improvements to health and well-being. These are just two examples but they help to reinforce the understanding and appreciation that there is more than just a tenuous link between mind and body – it is a very direct and close one.

The significance of this link is that it can be deliberately utilised to bring about serenity rather than, as is the case with the majority of people, leaving it to its own devices like a rudderless ship. So we need to find a way of harnessing body and mind and that way needs to be easy to do.

For better or worse – the marriage of mind and emotions

If there is a link between the body and the mind, there is an even stronger tie between the mind and the emotions. In fact, they are so closely intertwined that some schools of thought regard them as one. For our purposes, we can think of the mind as that which generates and experiences thought and perceptions and the emotions as those identifiable feelings that rise up and influence thought or arise as the result of thought.

For example, if we are angry about something, we are experiencing a certain feeling, that of anger, and we are also having a stream of thoughts which are negative in character. The two things, the feeling and the stream of thoughts, are separately identifiable as feelings on the one hand and thoughts on the other but can one exist without the other?

We can certainly think without being swamped by feelings, so thoughts in themselves do not depend on feelings or emotions; but can we have feelings or emotions without thoughts? Probably we can but not for long. For example, we might have a vague feeling of anxiety that we can't pin down a reason for but within a very short time either there will be a stream of thoughts arising from that feeling or our thoughts will be affected by it. Desires are another type of emotion and we may feel a desire arising and then the thought processes start to kick in. How strong the thoughts are will depend on the strength of the feeling of desire.

Thoughts can, of course, themselves evoke emotions. We might be thinking about something that has happened in the past or on some future event and feelings will arise based on the memory of past experience. Or someone might be talking to us and we might form a view based on our beliefs, prejudices or perceptions ("she has no right to talk to me like that," for example) and, whoops, up come the feelings.

The importance of all this is that it has a very direct bearing on serenity. If we want to experience peacefulness, we have to be able to do something about the emotional side of our nature. We have to be in charge of it rather than be ruled by it. This doesn't mean suppressing it but it does mean using our creative faculties and intelligence so that we can deal with feelings and emotions without being swamped by them. As the mind becomes calmer this becomes easier to do for two main reasons. First, because the mind is calmer and clearer, fewer emotions are evoked by the way we think; second, because mind and body are more settled, we are more aware of when an emotion is arising and more able to pacify it.

Why subtle energies are the key to our sense of well-being

Coursing through the body are numerous channels that carry the vital energy or life-force, or "chi", as it is often called. Chi provides the vital energy to the organs of the body (hence many of the meridians, the main channels, are named after the organs that they influence) and indeed to the whole body through a very complex network. When there are blockages in the network, imbalance results. If we think of the system that carries chi as a sort of bio-electrical circuit, we can perhaps imagine that if not enough current (chi) is running through certain parts due to poor circuitry there will be coldness and lack of energy there whilst there may be congestion and overheating due to overload in other parts. When chi is abundant, i.e. we have a good supply, and it is well-balanced, then health is good, the body is strong and we feel well.

As practitioners of chi kung and the internal martial arts know very well, chi can be "led" by the mind. In other words, we can influence the flow of chi by thinking or by shifting our awareness. For example, if we breathe with our awareness on the lower abdomen where a major energy centre for chi is located (the "lower dan tian") it is possible to feel the energy building up there.

Now, the reason that chi can be led by the mind is that there are corresponding subtle energies in the emotional and mental layers of our being and the relationship between these and the chi is very close. When we think, there is a movement of subtle energy in the mental layer or mental body, as it is sometimes called. If that movement is strong or maintained, it can significantly affect the flow of chi at the vital level of our being. In general terms, if the flow of chi is good, the blood circulation will also be good.

Bearing in mind the connection between the subtle energies or "winds" of the mind with the vital energy or chi of the body, it becomes easier to understand how upset in one can create upset in the other. If the mind is agitated, the energies in the body will be agitated. Similarly, if the body is upset or stimulated, it is likely that the mind will be unsettled too. So when we talk about becoming tranquil, we are not talking about just calming the mind; we are really talking about bringing a state of calmness to both body and mind because they are both interdependent.

The relationship of the breath to the subtle energies, to the mind and to the body

Most of us take the breath very much for granted. The only time most people think of it is when they are short of it or perhaps for a few seconds when they take a "breath of fresh air" after being in stale air indoors. I remember the emphasis on breath in biology lessons at school was about its role in carrying oxygen into the body, in taking carbon dioxide out of it and the function of oxygen in the body. But breath is far more than physiological respiration; breath is the magic bridge between body and mind and, as we shall see later, awareness of the breath is a major tool in bringing about tranquillity and, as a result of that, clarity of mind.

When we are feeling agitated or upset, something happens to our breathing. It becomes shallower and more rapid. We tend to breathe into the top of the lungs and the diaphragm goes up on the in-breath rather than downwards as it would do if we were calm. The heart rate is also higher and the body behaves as if the most important thing is to maintain a rapid intake of oxygen. It does this because adrenalin secreted into the bloodstream brings the body to a state of readiness for action – the "fight or flight" response.

As well as bringing oxygen into the body, the breath brings in chi from the air. Obviously the quality and quantity depends on the quality of air but the pattern of the breath also affects the flow of chi in the body. If the breath is shallow and rapid, it will tend to bring more chi to the surface of the body, away from the centre of the body where its presence helps to stabilise us. In effect, the chi is "drained off" to the surface and our calmness and stability disappear. Conversely, when the breathing is slower and deeper, the chi tends to build up in the centre of the body and in the energy centre known as the lower dan tian, in the lower abdomen just below the level of the navel. If the chi is settled and stable, the subtler energies it affects – the "mental winds" – will also be more settled and as a result our thinking is clearer and our emotions are steady. So the advice that is sometimes given to someone who is upset to "take some deep breaths" has its basis not just in physiology but also in the subtle energy system.

There are many systems of breathing exercise but we have to be very careful with them. If the breath were simply about oxygenating the blood and carrying away the carbon dioxide, there probably wouldn't be any need for caution, other than ensuring that we avoid hyperventilation or perhaps even hypoventilation. Without going into detail here, problems can arise because of the effect of the breath and breathing exercises on the chi. If we concentrate too much or overemphasise a certain aspect, we can cause the chi to accumulate and stagnate in a particular area. A lady who attended one of our tai chi classes made herself quite unwell for several hours because contrary to instructions she was attempting to do deep breathing whilst practising tai chi moves. So it is important that we are careful and to that end breathing exercises are not advocated in this book. However, we can still utilise the breath as a vehicle for harnessing the body, mind and subtle energies together to enhance our calmness, clarity and well-being and that's what we'll look at now.

An easy exercise in calming the mind and body through observing the breath

This exercise can be done standing, sitting or lying down but I recommend doing it seated to begin with. In fact, if done whilst seated it can be used as a form of meditation for quietening the mind and is probably one of the simplest, and oldest, forms of meditation; it is also extremely effective. Before beginning, place the flat of one hand on the lower abdomen, just below the navel or near the navel, and breathe out. As you breathe out, you should be able to feel the abdomen draw in slightly and, as you relax and breathe in, it should expand. If you find the movement is the other way round, it means that you are breathing in such a way that the diaphragm moves up rather than down on the in-breath which results in a shallow breath. Once you have become used to this exercise, you won't need to feel the movement with the hand but it's a good idea to do it the first couple of times just to become used to the movement. Now, once you have felt the movement, you can take the hand away and begin the exercise:

- *Sit up reasonably straight with the hands resting in the lap or on the knees or thighs. If you are sitting in a chair, make sure that the legs aren't crossed at the knees and the feet are flat on the floor. It's important to be comfortable but if we slouch, we constrict the energy channels in the body, especially in the back, and we won't have the same benefit.*

- *Place the awareness on the lower abdomen and exhale, feeling the movement of the abdomen.*

- *Close the eyes and continue to breathe normally, simply being aware of the movements that come with the breathing.*

It's important not to try to control the breath in any way; this is not a breathing exercise and we should be relaxed. If you don't like having the eyes closed, having them half closed with the eyes downcast is fine.

That, simply, is it. We should sit like this for at least five minutes and once we become used to it, a ten minute session will work wonders. When we find the mind wandering, we simply bring it back to the movement of the breath.

More on the law of cause and effect: How causes recorded in the subconscious affect our inner serenity

In Chapter 1, we looked a little at the law of cause and effect. All circumstances and all conditions have their preceding causes – they must have otherwise they couldn't exist – and anything we do, think or say produces an effect. If someone speaks to us in an offhand way, for example, and we react with irritation or even anger in our voice, it might well produce an adverse reaction in the other person and the situation may become a little heated. Even in this simple scenario, the causes could be quite complex. There must have been causes as to why the other person was offhand in the first place – how they perceived us, for example, and they may have been having a lousy day – and both of these causes would be the effects of preceding causes, and so on and so forth. The chain is virtually endless. And how we reacted would depend on how we saw the other person, how we were feeling etc. etc. Such things are not difficult to work out although we would probably never get to the end (or beginning) of the story.

There is a subtler aspect to this law, though, because it doesn't just operate on the physical level, in our everyday outer world. It also applies in the subtle world of our emotions and habitual thinking patterns and these are affected by, amongst other things, the seeds that are sown in our subconscious and in our subtle bodies. These seeds are responsible for many of the consequences that people sometimes put down to "karma".

If we do something that we know is wrong, an effect is stored in us. Suppose, for example, I take something that doesn't belong to me and when someone asks if I've seen it, I deny all knowledge of it. There are two "wrongs" there: the wrongful taking and then the denial. Because I know they are wrong, the memory of these acts is stored and it is interesting to see how they are stored. We might think that they are stored in the memory in the brain and that would be true; but the story doesn't end there because it isn't just the brain that stores memory. Our subtle bodies, the vital or etheric, the emotional and the mental bodies, consist of energy and memory is stored here too. We know that when we are generous and loving our energy goes outwards

– it radiates. When we act in the opposite way, the energy turns inwards; we "cramp our own style" because we create a knot or an implosion in our energy system. If the act is strong enough, there will be a very deep scar in our subtle energy bodies. These scars don't have to be caused by our own actions; we might suffer an emotional trauma or disturbance, but the important thing for us to understand at this point is that our own actions are recorded, so to speak, in various parts of our system, the brain being the outer level and our mental body the innermost.

If we act in a positive way, there is obviously a positive effect on our system and so it is possible for the negative effects, the knots and scars, to be neutralised. In the meantime, though, there is an effect on how we are and feel because the flow of subtle energies that course through the various layers of our being is adversely affected. At a subtle level of thinking, we know all is not quite right. This affects our sense of wellbeing and our perception of our world. Our happiness factor is not at its best.

What we have been talking about might be described as "mental karma". We reap what we sow in terms of how we feel inside. In order to neutralise this negative mental karma, we need to undergo a healing process and it seems that part of this healing process is that sometimes we have to experience the type of pain or suffering we have inflicted through wrong actions or wrong speech. It is as if we are drawn to situations where that might happen or where there is an opportunity to "put things right". In terms of energy, that makes sense. We are energy and if the energy needs to be put right, it will find a way to balance itself. Although it has received something of a bad press at times because it can be (and often is) abused, the practice of confession which is to be found in many spiritual traditions has its basis in healing the psyche in this way. It may not heal the wounds or undo the knots at all levels of our being but it certainly can help or kick-start the process.

On a more practical, everyday basis, what is important

is that if we know we have done wrong or made a mistake in some way, we try to put it right. That might simply be making a sincere apology or it could be making amends in some way. By making a genuine attempt to put things right (and we cannot always do so) we inject positive energy into the memory and so help to heal the negative imprint. It might be that we cannot do anything or apologise because we do not know or cannot contact anyone who was on the receiving end of what we did or said or it may be that to say or do anything would only make matters worse. In those instances it can be helpful to visualise a genuine apology; in other words, we imagine the other person (or group or whatever the "wronged party" is) in front of us and offer from our hearts a deep and sincere apology. Of course, the other party is totally unaware of this but we shift what can be a huge energy block within us. That can heal us and because of that it can also help to heal relationships.

The important message we really need to take on board if we are to attain a more tranquil or serene state of mind is that our whole being is a recording instrument and what it records affects our energy at all levels. How we think, speak and behave leaves an imprint which in turn alters the flow of our energies. Those energies dictate to a very large degree how we feel and how we react to those around us and our environment. They affect our mental state and therefore how we perceive things. Other people will sense whether our energy is positive and open or whether parts of us are closed off; so how we are inside will determine to some extent how others are with us. If we are positive and reacting reasonably well with the world around us, our energies will tend to be more settled and we will feel happier and calmer. If our energy pattern is chaotic, it will tend to draw us into situations where things often go wrong. So we need to avoid negative actions and negative ways of thinking. This is not an injunction to be angelic, but at least if we try to act and think ethically, we will be more comfortable with ourselves and life will be more enjoyable.

The nature of thoughts and habitual patterns of thought

Have you ever thought about your thoughts? From the moment we open our eyes in the morning until we close them and fall asleep at night, we produce an endless stream of thoughts. Perhaps it would be more accurate to say "streams" of thoughts because there appears to be little relation between many of them. But each thought we have is preceded by a thought or an event of some kind – the phone ringing, perhaps, or someone speaks to us or we hear a noise – and produces another thought. If all that thinking was effective and productive, what amazingly efficient beings we would be! Unfortunately, most of our thoughts are a waste of time and energy.

If we observe what we are thinking about, we will probably find that at least 90% is about what has gone on in the past or what we think is going to happen in the future. In thinking about the past, we might be reflecting on what has happened, how we dealt with a situation, why someone spoke to us the way they did, what made so-and-so do this or that, what a pleasant evening we had last night and so on and so forth. That's human nature, isn't it? We also think about the future. What time we need to be somewhere, hoping something turns out ok, imagining how we are going to deal with a situation, how someone is going to react, looking forward to a holiday etc. It sounds exhausting and it *is* exhausting. Thinking uses up energy. It uses up physical energy in the form of calories (a good thing, you might say) but too much thinking also dissipates our chi and other subtle energies resulting in our awareness lacking focus and coherence. Thinking can stir up emotions, too. Everything seems hunky-dory and all of a sudden our mind flits back to a painful event in the past – and *whoosh* – up come all the old emotions; or we start to worry about what might happen in the future.

All this is truly remarkable because the one thing we are not thinking about very much is what lies between the past and the future – now. All we have, ever, is the present moment. There is nothing else. Life is just an unfolding present moment but if we are not present *in* the present, life is lost to us and we are lost to life.

Even listening fully to someone is difficult. With every good intention we begin listening but how long is it before the mind wanders? Training is given to counsellors in how to listen because everybody is so bad at it. Within minutes or even seconds we will be thinking about what we need to do next or where we need to be; or what has just been said reminds us of something that happened to us or that we've heard about and so we are dying to find a point in the conversation to bring it in. If you're a good listener and this doesn't apply to you, well done; unfortunately, not many of us are good at it.

Because thoughts generate further thoughts, everybody tends to generate thought patterns. I had a few years of working with someone who had a razor-sharp intellect and a wit that was so fast that you could hardly keep up with it. His mind was in permanent overdrive and he admitted that he just couldn't stop. He would churn out reams of material for people to read on professional matters and he would work late into the night. Very few people had the time or capacity to read everything he produced. His mind was like a flywheel that had developed such momentum that tranquillity was an entirely unknown experience. After a time, I noticed that my thought patterns were responding to his wit and so some very quick and sharp banter often came up between us. It was great fun at first but after a while it began to be tiring and the only way to stop my own thoughts going into overdrive when we met was not to respond to his quips and so not generate further repartee. Some eastern teachings on the mind and meditation speak of the mind as generating heat or fire and that the mind can become "too hot" from too much stimulus. In less prosaic language, we might say that the momentum of over-thinking can create tension in the mind which, if prolonged, destroys or prevents any sense of well-being.

To attain some state of tranquillity or serenity, it is important to cultivate patterns of thought that are predominantly positive and which tend to bring us more and more into living life fully in the present moment. This doesn't mean living an artificial existence where life is spent in a cocoon separate from everyone else, far from it. It means living a life of fullness and richness, a life where there is contentment from knowing that, whatever the circumstances, "right now" is right, now. That sort of outlook on what the world brings to us means that we don't have to look for satisfaction elsewhere and gloss, glitz and glamour are seen for what they are – a veneer and nothing more.

Quality of consciousness v. quantity of actions

What is more important – our consciousness or our actions? Society tends to judge its members by what they achieve and inevitably we are affected by that. Value is put on what people do and so life is dominated by an ethic that demands that we be doing something, all the time. That creates a pattern of thought in virtually all of us of "doing" and "being busy". (Admittedly there are some who reverse that into valuing doing as little as possible but they are the exception and most unlikely to be reading this!) Whether we spend our life running a home, studying, going out to work or caring for others, whatever it may be, in most of us there is a tendency to need to do things or need to be seen to be doing things. It becomes a habit. Many people who retire from work find that they feel they have to be doing something because that is the culture we live in. One man told me it took him five years after retiring before he could allow himself to sit and do nothing for a while without feeling guilty about it.

But is what we do always so important? Pareto came up with the principle that 80% of what we achieve comes through only 20% of our actions. From my observations throughout life, even that is optimistic for many people. Given that we spend so much time "doing", is life so much better for it?

If we look at the reason why we are here on the face of the Earth, we might come up with several answers. Some may say we are here to improve the lot of others, some may say our purpose is to love, others may say it is to learn and gain experience; a few, who perhaps haven't looked at things as deeply as they might, may say we are here by chance or accident. It is for each of us to find why we are here and the answer for each of us may be different in its detail; but the essence of all the answers must be that the reason we are all here is to evolve. That evolution must be to improve, widen, deepen and clarify our consciousness, a process that is often called "enlightenment". If that is the case, it must be that whatever we do should be done with the fullest awareness we are capable of because if our awareness is only partial and is on other things while we are carrying out an action, we are only living partially and our consciousness will not evolve.

That brings us back to the question posed a few moments ago – what is more important, our consciousness or our actions? The quality of our consciousness is the most important thing in any given moment and provided we look after our consciousness, the actions that we carry out will be filled with quality. As the song says, "It's not what you do, it's the way that you do it."

Please do not think that I'm encouraging you or anyone else to stop doing things. But it's better to do something well and with full awareness than to rush through half a dozen things with only half a mind on the job. Be fully aware in the present moment; be aware that you are alive and fully present and carry out whatever needs to be done with that quality of awareness. It may be that you will carry out fewer actions but you will be fully alive and that is what matters. This will bring calmness into life and gradually your life will become more serene. "Being" will become part of "doing".

Someone wrote years ago that the in-tray is never empty. There will always be something to be done. One day this life will be over and we won't be able to reach for the in-tray but what we will have with us is our consciousness. Will that consciousness be improved as a result of our life? At that point, that very final point, that is all that is going to matter.

An exercise in developing awareness of breath and body

We have already looked at the relationship of the breath to the mind and the body and how observing the breath helps bring about calmness and stability in the other two. The exercise that follows is the first of three further very effective methods we are going to look at in increasing those qualities. It works by heightening the awareness of body and breath and brings a calming and healing effect to the whole body.

- *Sit comfortably with eyes closed or half open. Allow the body and mind to settle. Be aware of the breath and let it follow its own rhythm.*

- *Now bring the awareness to the top of the head and smile. Be relaxed and feel as though you are "breathing a smile" into that part of your body.*

- *After a few moments bring the awareness to the eyes and the face. Do the same – be aware, smile and breathe.*

- *Move on to the ears and the back of the head and repeat the process.*

- *Gradually work down through the whole body, stage by stage, not forgetting the major internal organs such as heart and lungs as you do so, eventually ending at the toes. At each stage, be aware, smile and breathe.*

- *Finally, bring the awareness to the whole body and breathe and smile.*

This wonderful exercise can also be done lying down, although it is possible to drop off to sleep! Having said that, this is a very good thing to do in bed if there is difficulty sleeping. If, for example, you wake in the middle of the night and can't go back to sleep, just lie there and slowly go through this exercise two or three times. You may not even complete the third one.

In the sitting mode, it helps the mind to relax and expand and brings a greater broadness to our normal state of consciousness.

Developing calmness in body and mind – a simple exercise

At the end of the working day or at any point in the day when we are feeling some tension, five minutes of this little technique will refresh and restore calmness. If we make a habit of doing it on a regular basis, the benefits will build up.

- *Sitting or lying, be aware of the breath.*
- *On each in-breath, feel that you are breathing calmness into the body and mind. You can even have the thought, "Calmness is entering my body and mind."*
- *On the out-breath, feel all tension go out – "All tension is being released."*
- *Gradually feel a state of calmness and a letting go of all tension come over you.*

Get up from this very gradually and go gently into whatever activity you have to do – or just sit or lie and enjoy the moment and the peace.

How to contact the silence within the body

It isn't possible to experience the tranquillity or peace of any place unless we are in touch with our own inner, serene state. We can be in the most peaceful and beautiful surroundings, yet if we are feeling tense or stressed, tension and stress is the experience. The converse is also true – we can be in noisy surroundings and yet be at peace inside if we are in touch with our inner nature and can feel our own quietness.

The paradox is that there is silence within sound or noise and that sound emerges from silence. That isn't so bizarre when we consider that sound is only vibrations and that vibrations are carried through the air (or other medium, such as water) as waves causing a reaction on the membrane of the eardrum, which in turn sends a signal to the brain. The vibrations cannot reach the eardrum without the silence of air and it is the air changing from a state of stillness to one of movement that enables the vibration to be. And if we look at it a little more deeply, the vibration itself isn't sound – it only becomes sound when there is a reaction on a receptor, in our case the ear and the brain.

Listening for silence when there is sound is not a crazy thing; rather it is an extremely useful tool for bringing about and maintaining a serene state. This exercise of feeling silence in the body can be a huge help in developing this skill.

Feeling silence

- *Close the eyes and feel silence in all parts of the body. Go from part to part, in any order you wish, feeling the silence. Maintain some awareness of the breath but emphasis should be on the silence.*

- *After about 4 or 5 minutes, bring the awareness totally to the breath. Feel the silence of the breath itself as it goes in and out of the body for about another 3 minutes.*

Some people manage this quite quickly, whilst for others it may take several attempts before there is much progress. It really is worth persevering with because once we can hear the silence in the body, we can begin to hear the silence in our surroundings and in today's noisy world that truly is a boon.

Tips for bringing tranquillity into daily life

To improve the quality of life, there needs to be more than just an occasional top-up of greater calmness; there has to be some adjustment to lifestyle. The following pointers will help that adjustment to be made.

- *Practise one of the exercises we have looked at in this chapter, or something that is similar that suits and appeals to you, at least once a day.* This will provide a good base for calmness and will restore balance.

- *Slow down your activity.* Although it is not possible for many of us to slow down all our activity, it is surprising how much we can adjust and actually perform what we have to do better simply by slowing down. Sometimes do something deliberately slowly, in slow-motion almost, and this will help to break the habit of doing everything at a fast pace.

- *Slow down your thought processes.* Rapid-fire thinking is not helpful because it agitates the subtle energies and creates tension in the body. Try to think calmly and clearly and on one thing at a time.

- *Be aware of the breath as much as possible, even in activity.* This will help to slow the mind down and it will increase awareness. This doesn't mean we should concentrate on the breath – simply be aware of it in the background.

- Live in the present moment and do whatever is in hand with full awareness. If you are eating, for example, be fully aware of what you are chewing and not thinking about the next mouthful, the next course or what you have to do next. If you are listening, listen fully and give the other person your full attention without the mind wandering. If you are walking, enjoy feeling your steps.
- Smile. Smiling releases endorphins in the brain, increases the sense of well-being and helps to promote stillness. Just a light smile is enough – we don't have to walk round with a fixed grin!
- Ensure you have some time each day by yourself. For some people, that may not seem so easy but if we are constantly in the company of others, it drains the energy and keeps the mind over-stimulated.
- Do something that you feel good about each day. This helps build self-esteem and calms the mind.

Remember that quality of life depends not so much on external factors but on how we feel inside. The aim is not to become artificially still by cutting ourselves off from everything but gradually to bring more and more stillness into what we do. If we do that, we begin to touch the deeper parts of our being and operate from still waters rather than shallow rapids.

6

Deeper insight equals greater happiness

Why we need to change our perception of the world

Isn't the mind an amazing thing? It really is a magician that can pull together things that present themselves before our eyes and convert them into images. For example, a mass of tiny dots on a page is just a mass of tiny dots but the mind can put them together and see them as a picture. Pictures can be broadcast across the world and appear to the mind as images on television screens; but there isn't really a picture on the screen, just a mass of electronic signals. If the mind didn't work in this way, it would not be possible to communicate using images. If all we saw in an artist's painting were various coloured pigments, the work would be meaningless. And yet there is something of a deception going on because the mind is making out something that isn't really there.

If we watch a film, it is possible to become totally engrossed in the story and for a while the characters in it can seem real. The same can happen when reading a book, the only difference being that the mind works a little harder with the book to make images out of words. But in both cases, we can become emotionally involved in the story as though it were real.

What we are going to be looking at in this chapter is how the same principle of converting false appearances into reality is a trick that the mind applies to everything with the result that we are often led away from happiness and contentment. When we can see things for what they really are, we don't get lost in a mire of emotions. The world that we see is not the world as it really is; what we see is what the mind has intriguingly put together for us. And because we are all different with different backgrounds, beliefs and emotional makeup, each one of us sees a different world to everybody else. No wonder there are problems! But if we can make a move towards undoing some of the mind's trickery, our own problems become less and gradually disappear. No-one can do that for us but as the mind is the cause of all the complexity and error, we can use it to undo itself and, as it progresses, we develop deeper insight and greater happiness.

The world is nothing but a series of energy systems

When we are dreaming, everything in the dream seems real. It may all be rather bizarre but it seems real while we are in it. But when we wake up, we know the dream was no more solid than a phantom or a mirage and usually we forget it quite quickly, if indeed we remember it at all. At the time, the dream imagery, which has all been created by the mind, is as real to us as when we are awake and it is only when greater awareness comes to us with waking that we can dispel it as unreal. In the dreaming state there is awareness but not as great as when we are awake; similarly when we are awake there is awareness but not as great as in the enlightened state. There is as much a contrast between the degree of awareness of the average person and that of someone who is enlightened (or perhaps we should say more enlightened) as between the dreaming and waking states. The enlightened person sees a different reality and one of the differences is to see things as energy.

Our world seems very solid and real but science tells us it isn't. Everything that looks and feels solid is made up of countless particles – atoms and molecules and the minute particles that make them up – and, just as importantly, the space between the particles. The physicist would tell us that the space between the particles is enormous – far greater than the "mass" of the particles themselves. The particles are whizzing round at enormous speed in a vast amount of space and this gives the appearance of solid matter. This means that when we look at or feel something solid, we perceive something that is not solid at all. It's an illusion.

Although it is impossible, unless we have exceptionally sensitive and subtle vision, for our eyes and mind to see solid things as mainly consisting of space, it is not a great stretch of the mind to think of things in terms of energy. In fact, all the particles are simply energy taking form and whether something appears solid to us or not depends on how densely the energy manifests.

The whole world is energy and that energy forms into billions upon billions of energy systems. You are an energy system, so is a tree, a bird, an ant and so on. All these energy systems are composed of billions of smaller ones; each organ in our bodies and every cell, all these are energy systems. Every family, community, anthill, shoal of fish, every nation; each can be described as a complex system or organism composed of energy. That means that everything is energy and everything is moving and vital. Nothing is dead because energy is dynamic. It's amazing if we take the trouble to think about it.

If we can begin to see everything in life as energy, we start to break down the concepts embedded in the mind that everything is solid and real. Try seeing everything as fluid and vital and gradually your perception will change and become freer. That's one stage; now let's look at another.

There is nothing to hold onto, so let go!

All of our emotional and mental pain and suffering comes from seeing things as real and solid. From this view of reality come two distinct states of mind; the first is attachment and the second is aversion. Naturally we desire to have or to hang onto those things and circumstances that we like. They give us pleasure and fulfil our desires. Understandably, we don't want to lose those things or circumstances. This is called "attachment" and it can result in pain because we fear losing the things that make us happy or we actually suffer when we do lose them. Aversion is the opposite state; there are things or circumstances that we don't like or don't want to have and we'll do what we can to avoid them. Aversion results in pain because we fear those circumstances or things coming to us or we actually experience them as real and unpleasant if and when they do occur.

An example of attachment is that we might possess an item that was a gift from someone close to us. If we lost it or broke it we would probably be upset and that would show that we were attached to the item. But it isn't just things we become attached to; we can be attached to people, places and circumstances. If someone we are fond of leaves us or dies, attachment will result in grief at the loss; if property developers erect buildings that obstruct a fine view we once enjoyed, we will be upset if we were attached to that view. So it goes on. These are just normal, everyday reactions to life's events; and it is easy to see that aversion is just the other side of the same coin. The point is that these quite normal states of mind do not bring us happiness but instead dole out a fair share of misery and in extreme cases result in addiction, obsession or hatred; and the problem arises in the first place because of our view of reality.

The answer to this predicament we all find ourselves in is to learn to let go. We have seen that nothing is actually solid – science clearly tells us that – and we looked very briefly in chapter 1 how everything is in a state of change. Everything will eventually slip away from us because nothing is permanent. Like the events in a dream or a film, nothing is as it appears to be. There are different ways of changing our perception of things; some of the classic teachings advise us to act responsibly and ethically but at the same time to look at everything as though it were a dream or an illusion. Another way is to regard our mind as like a cinema screen on which the images of life are projected. Whichever way we choose, the important thing is to learn to let go of things and circumstances because the truth of the matter is there is nothing there to hold onto. Circumstances never stay the same and objects are just particles of energy clumped together. A good way to begin to release our mental grip on things is to see their impermanence and what better way than to start with ourselves!

An exercise in acceptance of life's changes

There are really three parts to this exercise and each part can be taken individually. They involve visualisation – a mixture of memory and imagination. If you find it hard to picture things in your mind, don't worry; think about the things that are to be visualised and you will still gain from it. The first part is to visualise ourselves at various stages of life, the second is to do the same with regard to someone close to us and the third is to look at the circumstances of our life. The first two parts may seem a little gruesome towards the end but they are worth persevering with as they are very liberating. If you find them too difficult, though, leave those final bits out to begin with.

1. Seeing the impermanence of your own body

- *Sit comfortably with the eyes closed or half closed. Visualise yourself as a child. See how your body was then, how small it was compared to now. Bring in as much detail as you can.*

- *Then take yourself forward to the teenage years. How did you appear as a youth? How different were you from being a child? How much energy did you have then?*

- *No matter what age you are now, see yourself at various stages in life until you see yourself as an elderly person.*

- *Now see yourself as old and frail, nearing the time of death. The organs of the body are slowing down and starting to fail. Watch the body become ill and finally die.*

- *Observe how the body becomes cold and stiff. Then decomposition begins. Watch the body totally decompose (or if you prefer see it cremated and the ashes scattered). Be as vivid as you can in the imagination. Eventually there is nothing left at all as the body has returned to the elements from which it was formed.*

2. Seeing the impermanence of someone else's body

- *This part is the same as we have just done except we choose as a subject someone we know, and preferably a person who is close to us. Use the imagination to see them as a child and then go through the various stages of life to death and decomposition.*

3. Seeing the impermanence of our personal environment

- *Still sitting with eyes closed or half closed, bring to mind all the things that form part of your life: home,*

> *possessions, job or occupation, family, friends, social life, absolutely everything which you would consider as making up your personal environment.*

- *Now slowly look at each in turn, looking for what is permanent about it. When you are satisfied that there is nothing permanent in its nature and that sooner or later it must go out of your life, move onto the next. Continue doing this until you can see that there is nothing in your life that has any permanence about it.*

It is good to do this exercise every now and again and gradually we should begin to feel freer as the mind loosens its grip. There is nothing morbid or fatalistic about doing this; it is simply a method (and a very old and well-respected one) to undo some of the fabrications of the mind and so bring about personal freedom. Enjoy it – and then let go!

When is a table not a table? Nothing is what it seems

As the mind is so adept at isolating one object from another and our own identity from everything and everyone else, it is hardly surprising that the world is so full of conflict and misunderstanding. Yet it needn't be so and the mind is doing us no favours by deceiving us in this way. If we take the time and trouble to look at things a little more carefully, however, we can see that nothing is isolated at all. In fact, we can see that everything is dependent on everything else for its existence.

Let's take a wooden table as an example. A wooden table is a wooden table because we recognise that it is made of wood, has a flat surface that objects can be placed on and has a number of legs or perhaps a pedestal instead of legs. In other words, we call it a table because of its appearance and function. Some years ago, my wife bought a wooden object with a circular, flat surface, a central piece as a leg and a base shaped like two shoes. I was certain it was a stool but she was convinced it was a small table and it is actually used now as a side-table. So it is a stool or a table? It depends on how we label it.

More important than semantics, though, is to look at the nature of a wooden table itself. It is made of wood and it has a certain shape. Has it always been a table? No, because it was created. Will it always be a table? No, because one day it will rot, be broken up, burned or in some other way transformed or destroyed. So the table has no permanent identity or existence. We could say it came into being and one day it will no longer be.

Perhaps what we don't think about so much is that anything comes into being because of a coincidence of a number of factors. At the most obvious level, the table couldn't have come into being without wood and without somebody to put it together. The chain of causation, though, is far greater and is virtually endless. If we take the wood itself, it had to come from a tree which relied for its subsistence on soil, light, warmth, moisture and air. So it isn't an exaggeration to say that the table has within it the element of earth from minerals and plant material, the element of fire as warmth and light from the sun, the element of water as rain falling from clouds and the element of air from the atmosphere. If any one of those factors were missing, the table simply couldn't exist. Nor could it exist without the person who felled the tree and the chain of causation that led to his or her coming into being. By looking a little deeply, we can see that there are myriad chains of causation affecting the transformation of tree to timber, then to planks of wood and so on. The table couldn't have come into being without every single one of the causes being present. We can carry out a similar analysis with regard to the sawmill, the transportation of the timber, the design, the carpentry, the marketing and sale of the table, the coming into being of all the people in all the various stages – on and on it goes. The significant point is that the table is dependent on each and every factor. Without the sun, the table could not exist.

Without the mother and father of the carpenter, the table could not exist. This reasoning doesn't apply just to our table. It applies to everything in the world, in fact to everything in the universe. Everything depends on everything else. This is sometimes called "interdependence". Nothing is isolated. Nothing has its own separate identity and permanence; and that includes you and me.

So we can look at our table in two ways. One is how we have always looked at it – just as a table. The other is to see it in a deeper sense and to realise it is composed of numerous other elements or conditions – the tree, the sun, the sawmill, diesel fuel, soil, rubber tyres, a truck factory etc. etc. And the reason for looking at it, and indeed everything, in a deeper way is that it starts to open up our awareness and to free ourselves from the habitual constructs within the mind that prevent us from realising the true nature of the world around us and of ourselves. We begin to liberate ourselves from narrow thinking and life starts to become richer as we increasingly appreciate the world about us and everything in it. Perhaps we might start to see that everything in this extraordinary world of ours is absolutely remarkable and a miracle in its own right.

An exercise in contemplating the true nature of things

You might say, "This is all very well and interesting but I have a life to live and wouldn't get anything done if I stopped to analyse everything like that," and that would be right. It isn't necessary to analyse everything but it is important to realise the principle. What is extremely helpful is to spend a little time now and again to pause and look at perhaps just one thing deeply. Here is a suggested way of doing that which you could adapt to suit yourself:

- *Sit comfortably and hold or have in front of you an object of your choosing (it could be as mundane as a pen or something more elaborate, such as an ornament). Spend a minute or two examining it closely.*

- *Now think about how it came into being. What is it made from? How did those materials come to be? What conditions or causes came together at various points in time to result in the creation of the object?*
- *Follow all the main links in the chain of causation until you have found that the whole universe contributes to the object being as it is and where it is right now.*

Allow yourself sufficient time to do this exercise thoroughly and without rushing. When you have become used to this approach of looking deeply, you will find that you can do it at odd times during the day without sitting down for a formal contemplation.

Who am I? How to begin an investigation of why we are not who we appear to be

The exercise we have just looked at can be done in respect of anything. If we look at ourselves, for instance, we will see without much difficulty that our body and our circumstances depend on chains of events and causes that are beginningless. The yearning and inquisitiveness that have spawned the popularity of genealogy are a reflection in a way of the desire of people to know their own nature. But there is far more to our existence than a lineage of ancestors. A family tree is just evidence of one particular line of causation. So many factors have contributed to our being in human form and being physically present in the place where we are at this very moment: parents, grandparents, teachers, friends, shopkeepers, manufacturers, farmers and so on as well as all the elements of nature. All these things, and goodness knows how many more, are in our make-up. Like the table (or anything else that can be perceived through the senses) our presence and our attributes are the result of certain conditions coming together at the right point in time and space.

If we begin to look a little more deeply at ourselves, beyond skin, flesh and bones, we will find that there are certain characteristics that could be said to make up our personality. At the outer level is the physical body and its energy systems and then there is the level of emotions and feelings. Our perceptions – how we see the world around us from the signals coming through the senses – form another cluster in our make-up and then there are the thought patterns, beliefs and prejudices that govern how we respond to the world. Underlying and embracing all these is an awareness or state of consciousness – the experiencing awareness. Each of these levels or aspects is interdependent on other conditions and if we care to look at them in a systematic way, a great change in outlook takes place. We begin to realise that our own nature, what we *really* are, is vast, incredibly profound and marvellous.

To contemplate this makes a wonderful meditation and here is one method of doing so, although you can adapt it how you wish. Of course, you may choose not to meditate formally, in which case just thinking through the general approach will still produce results. The important thing is to become used to this inward looking to bring about a change in our "mindset" – doing it once and then forgetting about it will not, I am afraid, achieve a great deal.

"Who am I?" – a meditation

- *Sit easily with a gentle awareness of the breath until you feel settled.*

- *Bring the awareness onto the body. Realise that the body is the result of many conditions coming together: your parents and a beginningless line of ancestors, food and drink, the environment, air, moisture, warmth and so on. The body consists of cells that are continually being replaced, most of which are no more than a few weeks or, at most, months old. The cells are composed of molecules which consist of particles and space. The body is not you; you are not the body.*

- *Now bring the awareness onto the feelings or emotions that are present now. They may be positive or negative; they may even be neutral. They may be clear or vague. Realise that all feelings are temporary; conditions cause them to arise and then they disappear; just like clouds in the sky, they come and go. These feelings present now are not you; you are not these feelings.*

- *Be aware of the messages you are receiving now through the senses and what your mind is making of them – perceptions. Perceptions are the interpretations the mind puts on the signals from the senses and then labels as various sounds, smells, sights etc. Realise that all perceptions are temporary. The perceptions you have now are not you; you are not these perceptions.*

- *Now bring the awareness onto any habits of thinking, prejudices and how the mind construes things and reacts. Realise that all thoughts arise from conditioning of the mind – experiences, education and so on – and that as your understanding and experience grow, so your mental conditioning changes. Your thoughts are not permanent. Thoughts that arise in your mind are not you and you are not the thoughts that arise in your mind.*

- *Take a moment now to be aware of your consciousness. This is your general state of awareness. Your consciousness now depends on your body, your feelings, your perceptions and your thinking patterns combined with a basic or primordial awareness. Your consciousness therefore fluctuates as the various conditions fluctuate and is temporary. You are not your consciousness.*

- *Now ask yourself, "Who am I? Where is the "I" to be found?" Then just rest in awareness.*

The extraordinary mystery of Being

If you carry out this meditation, or something similar, you will find (or should I say "you will not find"?) that your being, your essence or your nature, is a little elusive. Like a slippery worm, you might think you are approaching it and can grasp it, but then it slips out of reach. The "I" is nowhere to be found and what remains is beyond the intellect, that thinking faculty we have which always wants to grasp things and label them as "this" or "that". People have tried almost since time began to describe "being" but descriptions require language and language is a product and tool of the intellect or logical, reasoning mind. To identify something, the intellect needs to understand what qualities a thing has and, just as importantly, the qualities it doesn't have. It needs be able to discriminate and to label things. Because it is beyond thinking, rational mind, Being cannot be described, it can only be experienced.

How can we experience something that seems impossible to identify? Only by going beyond the intellect. We have to transcend the everyday, thinking mind and simply "be". So simple in theory, it is very difficult in practice because we are addicted to thinking. Thinking creates movement in the mind and movements in the mind create more thoughts. It's a vicious circle but one that we have to go beyond or break out of if we are to know our true nature. That nature is happiness or rather happiness is what leads us to it because true happiness arises as we let go of things.

So is Being simply letting go or an absence of thinking? No, but it can only be experienced consciously as a state of pure awareness when conditions are right. Absence of thought and letting go of all concepts are two of the mental conditions that are necessary. It is also necessary for the nervous system and brain to be in good condition and for the subtle energies of the body to be flowing well. These are beyond the scope of this book and require years of training and dedication but they *are* attainable by anybody who genuinely wishes to apply themselves to that process.

But it is possible without years of training, and this is what this book seeks to assist the reader to do, to bring the mind *closer* to its true nature and in doing so generate the causes and conditions for happiness. As we do this, we draw a little nearer to unravelling the mystery of Being which is so succinctly and beautifully expressed in the injunction to "Be still and know that I am God." Or to put it another way, "Be still and know yourself."

How looking deeply heals negative emotions and leads to a happier life

Even though we might be making progress on improving our outlook on life, becoming calmer, clearer and so on, we will still find from time to time that we will be affected by emotions or feelings that we would rather we didn't have. We might be as "happy as Larry" one moment and then something someone says or a memory rising to the surface triggers something off and our calm, serene state seems to desert us. Feelings of anger, hurt, jealousy or strong desire are some of the stronger feelings that can arise without warning but there are sneakier variants to watch out for. Feeling resentful or even a little sulky, for example, may be less damaging in their effects but they still take away any possibility of happiness whilst they are there. There are scores, if not hundreds, of milder versions of the more obvious negative emotions and you would have to be more than a saint not to encounter them from time to time and some people might say they have them much of the time.

So negative emotions and the thoughts that they generate can be a problem for all of us but looking a little deeply when they arise helps us to cope with them and to start healing them. One of the fundamental things we need to grasp is that emotions, good or bad, are only temporary in nature. The same goes for thoughts. Emotions and thoughts are a little like clouds moving across the sky. There is no such thing as a permanent cloud and there are no emotions or thoughts that are permanent either. Our state of being, our true nature, is rather like the cloudless sky – boundless and ungraspable. Our thoughts and emotions scud across or may last for a period of time but they will eventually pass. They can only arise or exist when the conditions that support them are fully present. Those conditions are a mixture of perceptions, memory, experience and so on. The really important thing to understand is that emotions are not our true nature; rather they are in a sense *projected onto* our nature like pictures being projected onto a screen. The person who says, "I can't help being angry because that's the way I am," is denying the truth about himself. It might be that he experiences anger more often than some but that anger can only be there while the conditions are present for it to exist.

If we can recognise the nature of emotions when they arise, we can quickly take the energy out of them. Instead of indulging in the emotion or trying to suppress it (either of those actions will tend to strengthen it) we simply think or say to ourselves, *"I am aware of this feeling of ………. This feeling is not me, it is not mine, it is not my self. It is temporary and will pass."* Keep repeating this to yourself without fighting the emotion. Gradually, a sense of detachment will start to develop and the emotion will subside. By getting used to doing this, a healing process will start to take place and the emotion will, over a period of time, become weaker and weaker.

To finish this chapter, here is a meditation in the same vein which, when practised from time to time, strengthens our natural ability to heal ourselves:

- *Sit comfortably with eyes closed, gently aware of the breath.*

- *After a minute or two, become aware of any emotion or feeling that is present. It doesn't matter whether the feeling is positive or negative; it may even be neutral.*

- *Smile to the feeling as though it were an old friend (this may sound odd but it really helps).*
- *Realise that the feeling arises from conditions. It doesn't arise by itself anymore than a cloud can appear in the sky without heat, moisture and air currents. The feeling arises from the way you see things because of memories, past experience, the way you think or believe and so on.*
- *See that the feeling has no nature of its own. It isn't solid anymore than a cloud is solid. Like mist, it has no substance. It is empty and devoid of any true nature.*
- *Now think or say to yourself, "This feeling is not me, it is not mine, it is not my self. It is temporary and will pass, just like a cloud." Repeat this several times.*

7

The secret power of compassion

The incredible, dynamic nature of compassion

Compassion is extraordinary. It isn't a subject that attracts much attention and yet the transforming effect it can have is so powerful that it can change an individual for the better for the rest of his or her life. Perhaps that's why it isn't a hot topic – change is not something we adhere to very well. Not only that, it doesn't fill our pockets with money and, worse still, it involves thinking of someone else instead of ourselves for a while. How to have a simple life in the country, be self-sufficient and eat wholesome foods, give up the rat-race and not need much money – these are easier ways to attract someone's attention because they involve making the individual's own situation better. But beneficial though such subjects are, they do not carry a jot of transformative power compared to the possibilities for change that compassion generates.

Compassion has the power to change because it is dynamic. It releases something within us. It unleashes an energy that alters our perceptions and the way we think, it breaks down blockages of energy in our system at all levels and brings a sense of fulfilment that nothing else quite equals. In chapter 4 we talked about the amazing energy of love; compassion takes that amazing energy a step further.

Why wise compassion brings joy and completeness

If we made any progress on looking at our own nature in a deeper way as suggested in the last chapter, we may already be beginning to understand, or at least to accept, that at our deepest, most fundamental level we are not separate from anything or anyone else. At the deepest level, there is no "else". As we move a little closer to realising that in life, barriers and prejudices in our thinking and in our communications begin to dissolve and, as they do, joyousness and a sense of completeness become more real in our consciousness. A true and wise compassion speeds that process up. Instead of travelling by horse and cart, we have carbon-neutral jet propulsion.

What is compassion? It is *a loving, deep awareness of the suffering of others.* More than that, it is *coupled with a spontaneous desire to remove that suffering.* It is an attitude of total selflessness and yet it brings immense benefits:

- *It has a freeing effect because it involves a mental attitude of total giving.* To be truly compassionate, we have to let go of self-interest. In energy terms, that means we let go of all clinging or grasping and as we do that our energy channels become more open. Mental and emotional tension is released and that, of course, brings about the release of physical tension. We feel freer in ourselves because we focus less on our own problems or what we perceive as our problems and as we do that, they fall into perspective – they shrink in importance.

- *Compassion helps us in our relationships because we become less and less concerned with what we want out of them.* The same principle applies whether it is a close, personal relationship or whether it is a business one. Please don't think that we have to become fawning or obsequious – far from it; in fact, our outer behaviour may not change very much. The important thing is our attitude because that and the change in our energies will usually affect the other person in some way at a subtle level (they will often sense that our "vibes" are easier and stronger) and our own view of the relationship will be easier. Sometimes we may even find that a difficult relationship – perhaps where we wanted someone to be a friend, for example – is no longer something we need to strain to maintain.

- *Compassion can have a direct bearing on our health.* Both physical and mental health will tend to improve as we let go and start to give more of ourselves in this way. More endorphins, the "happy biochemicals", are produced in our system and stresses in life are less. As a result, the immune system tends to be stronger, quality of life improves and the prospects of life being shortened by stress are much reduced. We could say, therefore, that compassion is good for health, quality of life and longevity!

- *Compassion develops the heart energy centre.* The heart centre or *chakra* unfolds as we develop our spiritual qualities and as it does so, it distributes energy to the other chakras in a very natural and safe way. Those who try to "open their chakras" are often being misled by those who really ought to know better. Artificially trying to force our energy centres to open rarely works satisfactorily and can produce disastrous results. It is always safe to work with the heart by encouraging the heart qualities of love and compassion and the results are strong and stable, unlike those arising from some other methods.

These wonderful results come from a *wise* compassion. Being compassionate does not mean being soft or being a "do-gooder". A truly compassionate person is strong, stronger than most in fact, and is not someone who is prone to being manipulated. The compassionate person can say "no" when necessary because he or she doesn't have a hidden agenda which demands that the other person should be pleased. True compassion requires honesty and truthfulness. On the other hand, if to tell someone the truth is going to hurt, the compassionate person will strive to reduce that hurt to a minimum and will know not to say anything at all if it isn't necessary. To know which is right takes wisdom and wisdom comes from being in touch with our own nature. This doesn't happen overnight. Developing true wisdom and compassion is a task for life but every step on the way produces results. There are things on the way, though, that can trick us into believing we are being compassionate when we're not. Let's take a look at a couple of them.

Sympathy and pity are poor relations

If we think that because we have sympathy for someone or feel pity for them it means we are expressing compassion, we could be suffering from a little self-delusion. That doesn't mean to say that sympathy and pity are wrong things to feel – they are part of the range of human emotions that can arise when suffering is seen – but they do not evoke the same energy response in the heart. The danger is that if we do mistake them for true compassion, our old friend, the ego, will make a great deal out of them. For example, if we feel uneasy, or perhaps even a little guilty, at seeing a one-legged beggar in the street and throw him some coins because it assuages those feelings, that isn't compassion but our deluded mind, the ego, might persuade us that it is. When that happens, our progress grinds to a halt.

Pity is an expression of sorrow at the suffering of another and so we could say it is a good thing to feel. It is part of compassion as much as water is a constituent of tea but water is not tea and pity is not compassion. Why? What is the difficulty with pity? Pity is an attitude of mind that doesn't necessarily involve action and doesn't necessarily involve giving, although it can lead to both. We can feel pity at seeing the plight of someone else, whether it is a news report or seeing poverty with our own eyes. We may even be moved to give because it makes us feel better, as in our example of the beggar. That's pity and that's the reason many people in suffering resent the pity of others.

Sympathy is when we feel sorry for another's suffering. We may be at a loss as to what to do or say, if anything. We may send flowers, a card or do something else that helps to support the person who is going through difficulty. It may be there is nothing that we can do. Sympathy is perhaps a little nearer to compassion than pity in the context we looked at a moment ago but it doesn't involve the full energy of the heart. With sympathy or pity, there will be discomfort at the other's situation and wishing that it wasn't so but we may also probably be relieved that it's them and not us.

With compassion, we see the other person as ourselves and so there is a desire to alleviate the suffering and, at its deepest or strongest expression, a willingness to take that suffering on – in other words, "rather me than them" instead of "rather them than me". That's tough. But what it really means and involves is a letting go of all self-grasping. We can't actually take on the suffering of others. We can, though, let go entirely of "self". And as self-grasping is the root cause of all our own unhappiness, suffering and lack of fulfilment or contentment, that's not a bad thing to aim for.

Answering objections to the need for compassion

The mind will often raise objections to anything that involves letting go of self-interest and so it is almost inevitable that compassion will meet with resistance. Even if we accept the logic of how compassion works now, later some resistance will arise because it is easier to revert to old habits than engage in the discipline of mind that creates a new one. Because the mind is sneaky and devious, its objections will be dressed up as being logical and reasonable. Remember it is an expert at self-justification! So let's create a pre-emptive strike at some of the arguments the mind might come up with.

- *I don't have enough time or energy for myself now so how can I reasonably be expected to give what I don't have for others?* That sounds a reasonable argument. Most of us are pretty busy and could do with more time. But being compassionate is a state or attitude of mind and doesn't require us to find more time or energy. In fact, the compassionate outlook tends to make the mind clearer and as a result we have more energy. More often than not, what we see as pressure on our time is simply a result of a mind that is racing from one thing to the next and failing to remain in the present. No matter how busy we are, we can only act in the present moment and we never have anything other than the present moment. Only in the present moment can we love or be compassionate, only in the present moment can we find fulfilment. Of course, the ego might think we're too important for that!

- *If being compassionate is an attitude of mind, it isn't going to do others any good anyway.* Who says it isn't? Are there not some people you feel comfortable with and others you prefer to keep a distance from? Everyone radiates energy and people can sense, perhaps subconsciously, some of the qualities a person exudes. As the heart centre develops and we love more, become more caring and compassionate, we will be easier to be with. Truly, we start to improve our immediate environment. The compassionate heart also sends out a healing quality. That doesn't mean it cures the sick but it does help to create an environment where healing processes can take effect more easily. In short, the compassionate person helps to make the world a better place.

- *Isn't it hypocritical to have "good thoughts" for others just so that I feel better or happier?* It would be if that was our motivation but then we wouldn't be expressing compassion. Compassion is only when the concern is for the other person one hundred per cent. Its deepest expression is when there is a desire to remove the other's suffering to such an extent that there is a willingness to take that suffering on. In practice, another person's suffering cannot normally be taken on although, in a small way, we might be willing to endure a little inconvenience for someone else's comfort. The important thing is how the mind is and if we sense that we are being hypocritical, something is telling us that there is a little more work to be done.

- *I can't possibly generate compassion for people I don't know or care about.* So start with those you do know or care about. Rome wasn't built in a day and compassion isn't something that can be conjured up overnight. Once the feeling of compassion in the heart is recognised, it becomes easier to generate and there are ways, which we will take a little look at in a moment, to train the mind to see other people, known or unknown, in a different light.

There is no logical reason not to generate a compassionate heart. If you find yourself objecting or resisting, it is just the ego have a little poke at you to defend itself. Just smile at it and get on with it. There is nothing to lose and everything to gain. "All that I give, I give to myself," is an old affirmation that bears so much truth. Happiness is our goal but we have to lose sight of happiness for ourselves in order to arrive at it.

The importance of starting to see others as equal

The enemy, the only enemy, is in our own mind because the only thing that can really rob us of inner peace and happiness lies in the mind. It is the mind that creates all our perceptions and governs our thinking and our emotions. All unhappiness that arises in anyone has its roots in the mind. It arises because since time began we have been sifting things into categories. There are two basic categories from which everything else flows. The first category consists of the things, experiences, impressions and so on that we like; the second is the opposite – the things we don't like. These two categories have their extreme states, such as hatred and desire, which are easily spotted but they also have gradations, some so subtle that we hardly notice them. Pride, for example, is obvious when it is strong but how about the simple and common act of deflecting or denying blame when we have done or said something wrong? We may even try to convince ourselves, "Well, it wasn't really my fault; if so-and-so hadn't done or said this or that, I wouldn't have had to do it....." Common, isn't it? It pricks our pride to admit being wrong.

Liking and disliking produces discrimination and, in our subject of compassion, this is highly relevant. We have different feelings and perceptions about different people and probably about different classes of animals too. There are some people we find likeable or attractive and there are others we probably find we don't like so much or at all. We may even find some people obnoxious or repulsive in some way or perhaps we disapprove of them. This liking and disliking need not be strong, it can be quite subtle. If we think this is not the case, it would pay to look at our reactions a little more closely because we are almost certainly kidding ourselves; alternatively, of course, we may be very saintly and already have very pure perception!

It's this sort of discrimination habitually occurring in the human mind that impedes or prevents the expression of compassion. For example, if an elderly person we know very well and are fond of is attacked and robbed in the street, we would almost certainly feel compassion for that person, wouldn't we? But would we feel the same degree of compassion, if any, for the robber? You might say, "Why should I?" The point, though, is that our heart opens in one direction and closes in another. Where it closes, the possibility of happiness also closes. Compassion doesn't involve approving wrong actions in any way at all but it is possible to feel compassion for both parties to the incident. The victim's suffering is plain to see and we would have to be pretty hard-nosed not to feel some compassion for her. On the other hand, the state of mind of the robber is probably such that he feels no happiness whatsoever and, with a little understanding of the law of cause and effect, we can be sure that he is creating the causes for immense suffering for himself in the future. That knowledge might provoke a response along the lines of "it serves him right and the more the better" but again we are closing the heart and producing an inward negative response that adversely affects us.

If we are really going to enjoy the fruits of a compassionate heart, we have to change our perception; and the first step in that is to develop a state of equanimity towards all people. Equanimity produces a peaceful mind and the starting point for that peaceful mind is to begin seeing all people as equal.

How can we regard all people as equal when the human race is so diverse? The answer is quite simple. No matter how intelligent or stupid we are, how wealthy or poor, healthy or sick, young or old and so on and so forth, at the deepest level of our being we are all the same. And whatever activity we are engaged in, whatever thoughts predominate in our minds, whatever feelings and emotions arise in us, the purpose of life is to find that deepest level of being and know our own nature. The one thing that motivates everyone is the desire for happiness and to find their inner nature, whether that desire is recognised or not. Nobody wants to be unhappy but everybody makes mistakes – mistakes of perception, of thinking, of speech and of actions. These mistakes prevent the realisation of happiness. Even the criminal mind is pursuing happiness, mistaken and distorted though it is.

Equanimity is about levelling out our conceptions of people. We have to stop judging others. In the last chapter, we began to look into our own nature and to see that we are not the body nor are we our feelings, our thoughts or perceptions. The same applies to any human being (or to any animal, come to that). There is no reason or justification to judge others. My true nature is the same as your true nature; your true nature is the same as that of someone on the other side of the world. Just recognise that; train your mind to recognise that there is no gap between one person and the next. Take a look at your hand; would it not be ludicrous if the thumb thought it was superior in some way to the fingers or if it thought more of the forefinger than the little finger? Take a look at both hands. Unless you are ambidextrous, one hand does more work than the other; which is superior? Crazy, isn't it but that's how human beings tend to think – that one is better or worse than the other. But all are equal and it is mistaken thinking to favour one over another.

How we can help heal ourselves through compassion

There is an extraordinary thing in the universe that could be called "the universal healing force". It's a certain something that helps to support forms of life and is sometimes termed "cosmic glue". So long as a form, in our case the body, is helping consciousness to evolve, the universe will support it. This healing force isn't somewhere outside that we have to go and look for, though; it is inherent in consciousness itself. It is an aspect of our inner nature. When we are given medicine that helps to cure an ailment, it works as and when it awakens the healing agent within us. Similarly, if we were to receive healing from a healer or practitioner, it would be effective if, and only if, it stimulated or invoked our own inner healing response.

The key that accesses the healing force is love and compassion. We can only understand love, if we understand it at all, from the standpoint of our limited consciousness and experience and it is impossible to comprehend the extent of love and compassion of those whose consciousness is much greater than ours. Evolution is limitless and as love and compassion grow as we evolve, the possibilities for their expression are extraordinary. The possibilities for healing are therefore also extraordinary so long as we remember that forms, i.e. bodies, are here to serve a purpose for a limited length of time and that healing is to help that happen, not to extend life in a physical body indefinitely. You may recall that in the story of the Flying Dutchman, the eponymous hero was not a happy one!

Compassion, as we have said, means having our sights on the benefit and welfare of others rather than ourselves; so can we heal ourselves through compassion? The answer is "yes" on two counts. First, by exercising compassion towards others the healing force is naturally awakened within us. Second, it is possible, and legitimate, to be compassionate towards oneself and so release negative feelings and attitudes in self-perception. This second point is actually extremely important because how we perceive and act towards others is directly affected by how we see ourselves. The little exercise that follows is very helpful in improving self-perception. It helps to generate compassion and is a great healer; it is sometimes a good idea to do this exercise before attempting to generate compassion for others, particularly if we are struggling. It is based on a Tibetan practice of "*tonglen*" – giving and receiving.

An exercise in compassion towards ourselves

- *Sit somewhere comfortable where you won't be interrupted or disturbed. Using your imagination, visualise looking down on yourself from above and see that this "you" has suffered in the past in many ways and the traces of those sufferings still affect the way you see the world and interact with it.*

- *Now see those sufferings and any negative tendencies you may have emerge from the "you" like dark smoke. With your compassionate heart, as you breathe in draw this dark smoke into you the observer and transform it in your heart into loving kindness. As you breathe out, send this loving kindness to the "you" below, filling it with light and radiance. See "you" starting to smile. Do this for a few minutes until you feel a sense of ease within yourself.*

Healing relationships through compassion

It would be marvellous if all relationships were filled with love and happiness all the time but unfortunately that isn't the way of the world. Difficulties can and will arise from time to time. Relationships need not be close or personal either; families, lovers, partners and so on are obvious examples but whenever we have dealings with someone else a relationship is formed, however long or short. So they arise in business, in work, with neighbours, with people in the same club or society and so on; the common thread with all of them is that two or more human beings are interacting with each other. It's important to recognise this because each and every interaction with another human being provides an opportunity for growth. That isn't to say we should make heavy weather of relationships as that can be a recipe for disaster; if anything, the opposite is true because if we deal with people with a kind and compassionate attitude, relationships become lighter and easier. It is logical, too, to see all relationships as important if we have taken to heart the argument for equanimity.

In spite of good intentions, however, sometimes things go wrong and one person can see the other in a negative light. One may have said something that upset the other or acted in a way that meets with disapproval. There are a million and one ways of upsetting someone! Often things are put right with a simple apology, a discussion or an expression of love or friendliness but there are many times, too, when matters are allowed to fester. This book is not intended to provide advice or guidance on how to talk to people or how to resolve difficulties. What can be stated, though, is that it *is* possible to change how *we* are inside; in other words, we can change *our* attitude and *our* energies so that from our side there is no negativity. Often the situation will ease when we do that; sometimes it will remain the same, outwardly at least. At a subtle level, though, the other person will more often than not detect a change in the energies of the situation, albeit subconsciously.

From experience, I can say that the results can occasionally be remarkable. A person I knew once through work thought (quite wrongly) that I had schemed against her. Up to that time she had always been friendly but suddenly she took an intense dislike to me and became very cold. It was only later on that I discovered why she was acting in this way. If looks could kill, I would have died a thousand times! Then I didn't see her for quite a while but one day we found ourselves seated near to each other at a concert. She had shunned me outside, which I didn't have a problem with, but I thought it was so sad that she was obviously feeling very bitter inside.

Whilst we were in the hall waiting for the concert to begin, I practised *tonglen,* "giving and receiving", for several minutes. In the interval, she came up to me in the foyer and started talking to me in a pleasant way as though nothing had ever happened. It was astonishing because she hadn't spoken to me for a couple of years. Some sort of healing had taken place. It doesn't always happen like that but that isn't a rare example by any means.

"Giving and receiving" is so simple to do, yet it is extraordinarily effective. In some Tibetan Buddhist traditions it is part of the main practice because it is so transforming but anyone of any persuasion or culture can do this and benefit hugely.

"Giving & receiving" – a very effective healing exercise

- *This can be done anywhere or at anytime. Preferably sit somewhere comfortable where you won't be interrupted or disturbed but otherwise do it wherever you feel is suitable.*

- *See in your mind's eye the person with whom you wish to practise this. He or she has suffered in the past in many ways and the traces of those sufferings still affect the way he or she sees the world and interacts with it.*

- *Now draw those sufferings and all negative tendencies from this person like dark smoke. As you breathe in, draw this dark smoke into your heart and transform it into loving kindness. As you breathe out, send out this loving kindness, filling the other person with light and radiance. See him or her starting to smile. Do this for a few minutes if you can.*

This has been presented as something done towards an individual but it can also be done with a group as the subject. As we feel more comfortable with the process, we can extend it as widely as we wish. There is no reason why at some stage we should not be capable of including the whole of humanity in it but it is better to start in a small way and work up gradually. As we do extend it, though, we will feel a greater benefit.

What is the difference, you may ask, between this and the exercises suggested in chapter 4 where we visualise giving love and happiness? The essential difference is the aspect of compassion which not only wants to give but also wants to take away. You can't have compassion without love but compassion adds something extra to love. The extra something is the desire to remove suffering or unhappiness from someone else. You can love someone very much and feel really sorry for them when they are ill or unhappy and that is good; but if you have the attitude that you wish you could take their suffering on yourself so that they can be happy, you have compassion. You have gone the extra mile.

A powerful exercise in generating a deep, full heart

We talked earlier about equanimity – seeing everyone as equal – which helps to level out our conceptions. A common difficulty that most of us need to overcome at some point is not so much the negative feelings we may have towards an individual we don't like; that tendency is easy to spot and we know we need to deal with it. A greater challenge to us is to overcome indifference, the completely neutral feeling that most people have towards people they don't know; and as there are an awful lot of people we don't know, that's a big chunk of indifference. It's like having a sky that is interminably grey and overcast, dulling our perception of most of humanity. Would it not be better if our perception of humanity, and indeed of everything, were bright rather than dull?

The reason we have this indifference is that we don't have any sort of relationship with the people we don't know. Although that's an obvious point, think of some of the people you know or have known and how your feelings towards them were before you knew them and how they are now. When we form an acquaintance, the other person doesn't change but our outlook changes once we begin to have some rapport with them. As our quest for happiness involves changing our perception and as happiness doesn't thrive in dullness, we have to change how we see other people. That change can be brought about by using the imagination, which is a very powerful tool for altering the mind and our habits of thinking.

One of the most powerful techniques I have come across is to see people *as if* in the past they had been very close to us and shown us the greatest love, caring and kindness. It really is very extraordinary how a little change of view by using the creative imagination can affect our energy, and it can affect us very deeply. A word of caution – this is a very private matter. If you want to use this technique, please do; the transformation it can bring about is enormous. But if we start throwing our arms around people who haven't a clue who we are or even if we start telling people what we are doing, things will not go well. Keep it to yourself. Having said that, use it freely, go wild with it – *inside*.

This is a method *par excellence* for deepening the heart. The heart will begin to radiate great warmth, both throughout your whole being and around you. You will change. You will like yourself more and you will like others more. A deep warm heart is comfortable anywhere and feels safe. You will exude a quiet confidence, but not from any sense of self-importance or even of achievement. It is the sort of confidence that radiates from a true sense of humility and gratitude, from an appreciation of being alive and from having a deep respect and love for humanity.

If that sounds too big a step, don't worry. We only do this in small steps and you can stop whenever you want –

but you probably won't want to once you have experienced the effects. We start in a very small way and, if you don't want to take it further, that's fine; even a small step is a gain. But in all truthfulness, it is something that needs to be worked at because our habits of thinking are so deeply ingrained that it is easy to slip back into indifference. I want you to experience great joy and to have a life that is deeply fulfilling; but that's no good – *you* have to want it and it is only *you* who can do something about it, no-one else. This isn't something to read about, make a mental note of and then quietly forget. It is a technique and it has to be applied to make it work.

There are two parts to this. One is preparation by doing a little meditation. This helps to prepare the mind and it is a good idea to do the meditation now and again rather than as a "one-off". The other part is to use the technique in normal daily life and that is where the most benefits will be felt.

Preparation – a little meditation

- *Sit comfortably and easily where you won't be disturbed. Close the eyes and visualise in front of you someone you know quite well.*

- *Imagine that you have known this person before, in another lifetime, and that in that lifetime this person cared for you and looked after you. Imagine that perhaps as a loving parent, or whatever figure you feel comfortable with, this person gave everything to you and loved you very deeply. Allow your heart to soften.*

- *Now imagine that in this lifetime that special relationship has been forgotten but you want to repay the loving kindness that was given to you then by taking away all unhappiness they may have now and by replacing it with happiness. Spend two or three minutes, longer if you wish, contemplating this.*

You should, if you have used your imagination well, have felt a warm glow in the heart. Once you have become used to the idea, try using someone you hardly know at all as the subject of your meditation and then perhaps someone you don't know at all. The principle is the same; we are changing our view and allowing the heart to open to everyone. Time is not crucial to this – it is better to practise it a few times for a minute or two than to spend ten minutes and just do it once. Repetition helps to form a new habit and a new habit of thinking should be our aim.

Applying the technique in life

* *This reinforces the meditation. Whenever you encounter someone, even passing a stranger in the street, simply have the thought, "This person showed me the greatest possible love and kindness once and now I would like to repay it," and allow your heart to expand towards them.*

Don't make a meal of it, simply have the thought and let go. Do this as often as you can. Remember it is a mental technique with the specific aim of breaking down barriers within us. By so doing it allows us to express ourselves more fully and through that expression of our own nature, life becomes richer and deeply fulfilling. Bliss becomes a possibility; joyousness becomes a certainty.

8

Being happy – tips for a happier life

How we can help make a better world by being happy

Have you ever thought that being happy could actually be a responsibility? So many people describe our world as being in a terrible state, and it would be foolish to say that everything in the world is fine, but if it is in a terrible state, whose responsibility is it to put things right? Those who regard the world's condition as being parlous often put the blame fairly and squarely on governments, politicians and commercial interests. Rarely do they think that they have any direct responsibility or can have any effect themselves. But the truth is that all these organisations are comprised of people and every human being on the planet contributes to the state of the world as it is at any given moment through his or her consciousness.

If we think negatively, we contribute to the pool of negative thought. If we judge and criticise others, we add to the pool of judgmental thought that often breeds conflict. If we are extremely selfish in our thinking, we contribute to that tendency. However we think, we feed the pool of human thought.

Blaming a country's leaders or commercial corporations is to ignore the collective effect of human thought. Any government can only act according to the collective consciousness of the people it represents. If it tries to act against it, support for that government weakens; if the government tries to put into effect the will of its electorate, it will normally succeed. Where there is chaos and anarchy or a government is oppressive, it is because there is insufficient coherence in national consciousness. On the other hand, if a government is acting badly and the national consciousness is strong, there will eventually be a change of power, whether that is by democratic process or by rebellion. Commercial organisations may not reflect the will of the people but what they do reflect is the natural acquisitiveness of the human mind. They are there to make money and by and large people are attracted to profit and to possessions. Most commercial organisations actually serve the community in some way but where things go wrong it is because the drive for profit has overtaken the desire to provide useful resources. When they become out of hand, it is because human consciousness has allowed them to do so and caused them to do so.

The key to how our world is lies in the mind. How humanity operates depends on how everyone's minds are collectively. How we see the world depends on how our own mind is.

If the negative tendencies of the mind contribute to the things in the world that are not so good, it is obvious that positive thought can have an enormous impact too. It is here that the responsibility for being happy comes in. As we become happier, the negative trends of thought we may have in our consciousness diminish and so, in a very small way, we begin to purify human consciousness. Yes, it is a "drop in the ocean" but the "ocean" is important and what we do to it is important because we are a part of it. In fact the only way for the world to change for the better is by changing minds. Attempts have been made to do that by brainwashing and oppression and we see evidence of those in extremist organisations and in totalitarian governments. But that is not the way. The human individual has to be allowed to express his or her inner nature freely so long as that is not to the detriment of others. A human being is a spiritual being and the spirit must be allowed to emerge. That spirit emerges as a result of selflessness and the joy that comes from that, not from oppression. So the change of mind that must occur for the world to be a better place is an increasing altruism. That won't occur until there is a change of heart in every human being but it doesn't require an enormous effort, just increasing innocence and joy which come from letting go. As you become happier, as I become happier, those around us feel easier and happier too. Isn't that the sort of responsibility that we can take on without too much difficulty? Go on, enjoy yourself!

Improving potential for happiness through visualisation

Sometimes we have blocks to expressing happiness. These result from years of conditioning because, let's face it, life today doesn't prepare us very well for a joyous existence. The society we live in conditions us to be acquisitive; it conditions us to desire. In travels my wife and I have been privileged to enjoy in various parts of the world, there always seems to be a greater joyfulness from people in societies where material standards are generally much lower than in the West but where nonetheless there is a contentment with the social structure and culture that characterises them so strongly. Of course, they must have their problems but their outlook on life is more open and more accepting. Our western society, with some exceptions, is mainly conditioned to want, to be disappointed and to complain. If we were visitors from outer space observing this, we would probably double up with laughter because it really is extraordinarily comical in a sense – but it is also sad.

The point of these remarks is to recognise that it is a perfectly normal reaction sometimes not to be able to envisage ourselves as having the potential to be happy human beings. Inevitably there are what are sometimes called "mental formations" or ingrained habits of thinking that can militate against a happy response in us. In effect, these habitual thought patterns withhold energy; they cramp our style, so to speak. We could almost say they form a "repetitive strain injury" in the mind.

Visualisation is an extremely useful tool in overcoming these old obstructive habits of thinking. By using the imagination, we can forge new patterns of energy in our mental and emotional make-up and, as these become stronger, the old patterns gradually weaken. Some people say they find visualisation difficult, particularly those who "think in words rather than images" and have predominantly intellectual or analytical minds. It's true that picturing things in the mind uses the "right-brain" or the intuitive side more than the intellectual or logical side but gradually we can restore the ability, which we all had as children, to see things in the mind. If you find it difficult to picture things, simply have the idea or intention to see them and think about them without straining; it will still have the desired effect.

Two visualisations are suggested here. You can amend them how you wish to suit your circumstances. However you do them, approach them lightly. Please don't be grave or serious. On the other hand, a frivolous attitude isn't going to help either. Simply do them with, perhaps, a light sense of fun but also with the idea that they will help to ease and strengthen your energy and your life.

Seeing yourself as happy

• *Sit comfortably (or you can do this lying down) with eyes closed and allow the mind to settle. Being aware of your breath can help. Allow yourself to smile a little.*

- *Now picture yourself going through your daily life smiling and happy. Imagine yourself going through the normal dealings of your day with a warm, friendly heart. If you normally have difficult things to deal with, see yourself dealing with them with calmness and without agitation.*

- *See yourself greeting people in a friendly way and see them warming to your friendliness.*

- *Do this with as much detail as you have time for and be really relaxed about it. When you feel you have spent enough time on it, simply open the eyes, smile and gently stretch.*

You should feel quite good at the end of this but don't think that having done it once, that's it. The more often you do it, the greater the effect will be. A wonderful time to do this is first thing in the morning, before getting out of bed. But you can do it at any time and if you know you have a difficult situation to deal with, maybe a meeting you are not looking forward to, a few moments visualising yourself in that scenario in a happy, friendly and peaceful mode and seeing others warming to you will help strengthen you.

If we are rather serious in nature, we might think this type of exercise is too childish or even beneath our nature – but then the need is probably greater! In any event, if we use the strength of our logical mind to analyse the effect of mind and thought on energy, we will realise that those objections are baseless. There is a magic, too, in finding the innocent child within us. An important factor in following the path of return to happiness is re-discovering that innocence.

The second exercise helps to generate a sense of equanimity towards our surroundings. The human mind sees things in terms of positive, negative and neutral – "like, dislike and not bothered or don't mind." Seeing things in this way upsets our energy. Each time we find something that evokes dislike within us, for instance, our energy field changes and our sense of well-being dips. If we can see things as pure (and if we analyse everything deeply, there is nothing that is impure – what is impure about an atomic particle?) our sense of well-being will remain good. Actually to see everything as pure takes a great deal of time to cultivate but this following visualisation will assist in the process.

Seeing the environment as pure

- *First, with the eyes closed, bring to mind the environment you live and work in. Imagine that it is appearing like a magical display and that it is made from a very pure substance. Spend a minute or two examining how pure everything really is. Everything is just a manifestation of light and purity no matter what colours or shapes are formed.*

- *Now open the eyes for a few moments and look around. Apply the same thought: everything that is appearing is made from pure substance.*

- *Close the eyes again and imagine people appearing in your environment. Imagine that all these people are pure. Their bodies are made from pure substance and, whatever their outward appearance and actions, they are in essence pure, enlightened beings.*

- *After a minute or so, open the eyes, look around again and smile.*

Apart from easing our own internal energies, this exercise can help to begin purifying our perception. The whole enlightenment process, in other words the growth from limited perceptions and thinking to holistic thinking and experience, involves purifying how we see things. Joy arises in us as we move closer to seeing things as they really are rather than as we think they are. So although it may seem a great leap in imagination to see our environment as pure, all we are really doing is beginning in just a very small way to see things a little closer to how they really are.

Slowly, very slowly it may seem, we gradually train the mind to see a little more correctly. By applying these techniques, we can help to speed that process up and so markedly improve our potential for happiness.

Caring for our body: tips on energy and energy cycles

It's no use preparing the mind if we don't take care of the body, too. This isn't a book on healthcare but there are one or two things worth mentioning that are often overlooked or even ignored. As everything in our physical universe is energy in one form or another, we know that the energy in our environment affects the energy of the body. The body is not an insulated capsule; indeed, if we could see a very large magnification of the boundaries of the body, we might be surprised to see that the body's outline is blurred rather than sharply defined. It isn't overstating the case to say that the body isn't separate from the environment but is actually part of it.

Taking reasonable steps to ensure balance is not difficult; we know that the body is susceptible to heat and cold, to overexposure to the sun, to strong electromagnetic radiation and so on. So we simply have to make sure we have adequate protection from the elements and possible sources of harm. If we become paranoid about these things, though, (and a certain amount of fear is generated and bred by well-meaning factions, some official, some not) then we probably damage our well-being more than the supposed harmful environmental sources ever could. "Moderation in all things" applies here as it usually does to most things in life.

However, the purpose of this section of the book is not to go into detail about those things, which are largely common knowledge or can easily be read about elsewhere, but to give some brief information and tips on how we can co-operate with the *cycles of the Earth's energy* on a daily basis and so promote well-being and balance.

If we really listen to our body, this isn't difficult at all because the body will normally tell us what it needs. Most of us, though, probably don't listen as well as we should and many of us will probably only hear what we want to hear anyway! Once we understand a little about the cycles, we begin to appreciate the naturalness of them. Living in accord with them is perfectly normal and makes good sense. More to the point, we will feel good.

Three main areas of life, digestion, sleep and exercise, are particularly influenced and it is in these areas that it can help to make some minor adjustments unless, of course, our lifestyle reflects them already.

(a) Digestion

Digestion is greatly affected very much by natural cycles. The ancient Indian system of healthcare, *ayurveda*, regards the strength of the digestion as paramount in maintaining total health and vitality. All of us have probably had the experience of eating a heavy meal late in the evening and feeling it lying on the stomach throughout the night. The body does not feel at its best in the morning because there is an undigested residue in the stomach and because the job of the liver has been interrupted.

The power of the digestion is said to rely on "digestive fire", a prosaic but very apt description of the ability of the body to metabolise food. If our food is fully digested, we could almost say that we have a "clean burn fire"; but if there is only partial digestion, residues are left behind and these residues form toxins that stay in the body.

The analogy of a fire is a very good one. If there is a strong fire, more fuel can be added and it will be burnt easily, so producing heat; but if we put on a lot of fuel when the fire is low, it will smoulder without much heat and produce a deal of smoke, soot and tar in the process, probably leaving a quantity of unburnt fuel too.

The trick with our digestion is to know when the digestive fire is strong. A healthy appetite can be a good indicator if our eating habits are good. Unfortunately, confused messages often reach the brain so that there may be false sensations of hunger or appetite. These can be brought on by habit, by false stimulation (alcohol can artificially increase our desire for food, for example) or by insufficient intake of fluid which can lead to an empty feeling.

The normal daily digestive cycle of the body largely reflects the diurnal rhythm of our environment and is affected by it. Our digestive fire will normally be strongest around midday when the sun is at its highest. Like the sun, it will be rising but comparatively low first thing in the morning and again will be lower in the evening.

If we can respect this cycle, our body will follow more natural rhythms, our digestion will be stronger and our sense of well-being will improve as we produce less of the toxins that can result from poor digestion. Contrary to the adage to "breakfast like a king", respecting our digestion means that breakfast should not be huge or heavy as this will tend to dampen the "fire" before it has had a chance to get going; adequate but reasonably light and easily digestible should be the key.

The main meal of the day is best taken at lunchtime when the digestive fire is naturally at its height and the evening meal should be relatively light. For many people that is easier said than done, particularly if they are out at work all day. If the evening meal has to be the main meal, then at least try to be kind to the digestion and not make it too heavy nor have it too late. I have known a number of people in the business world who used to skip lunch, often boasting that "lunch is for wimps" and that they were too busy to eat then. Actually, they were quite unhealthy specimens who built up quite a bit of fat around the midriff because they were snacking on biscuits and then eating a very substantial meal in the evening. What they were doing was weakening their digestions and piling food in when the metabolism was low. Using the fire analogy, doing that is rather like putting wet logs or coal dust on a few gently glowing embers.

Apart from the daily digestive cycle which reflects the heat and light cycle of the environment, the body starts a cycle of its own once food is taken in. We could call this the small digestive cycle. In the small digestive cycle, the body secretes various enzymes at different points. If we put in more food before the cycle has been completed, it is rather like opening the door of the washing machine to stick in more dirty clothes before the first load has been washed, spun and dried. What happens? Because the process is interrupted neither intake of food is completely digested and toxins are left behind in the body. In a healthy individual with a normal appetite, the body will usually take at least six hours to digest a substantial meal (possibly longer if a lot of animal protein is taken) and even about four hours for a light meal or snack. These times will vary between individuals but they are a good rough guide. Having a warm drink will usually quell the slightly empty feeling that can occur when a meal is partly digested but a piece of cake with that cup of tea a couple of hours after a meal is generally not a good idea. Some people with medical needs, those with diabetes for example, must of course follow the professional advice they are given but otherwise respect your stomach and it will respect you!

(b) Sleep

"Early to bed and early to rise," and "An hour of sleep before midnight is worth two after midnight." Remember those sayings? They are actually truer than we might realise.

Linked to the daily cycle of "fire" are the cycles that are relevant to sleep. The traditional elements of air, water, fire and earth do not stem from ignorance about the existence of chemical elements but arise from observing the different aspects of nature. The fire element obviously represents warmth or heat together with light but also, as we have seen, represents metabolic processes. Earth element represents the solid or heavy aspect of all phenomena, water the fluid aspects and air represents lightness, movement and, obviously, anything gaseous. Sometimes a fifth element, space, is added because everything that exists has to have space in order to be.

The four main elements have their daily and seasonal cycles. The seasonal cycle is easier to identify, perhaps, as there are usually hot and cold seasons or, in some parts of the world, wet and dry seasons. For example, in winter fire is obviously at its low point and if the weather is predominantly dry and windy, water may also be low but air is predominant. As spring approaches with its time of growth, earth and water are strong and fire is slowly beginning to "wake up". In the summer, fire is at its peak.

In the daily cycle, we have seen that the fire element is strongest at midday; it is also strong twelve hours later, from roughly 10 p.m. to about 2 a.m. During this time our bodies make use of it but not for having a midnight feast; rather it is the time when some of our glands, especially the liver, are making use of the natural strength of the metabolism to process and detoxify. To do that job properly, the body needs to be at rest. If we stay up late and also if we eat late, the liver and kidneys have a tougher job on their hands and less time to do it in. The unfinished job means that we won't feel very bright in the morning and gradually the system becomes more sluggish. That's one reason for retiring at a reasonably early hour. Another is that the fire element tends to sharpen the mind, aiding the processing of thought, so sleep tends to be more settled and of better quality if it begins before the fire element is strong. Stimulating the mind with reading or television late in the evening disturbs the subtle energies of the body and leads to poorer quality sleep.

From about six o'clock to around ten in the morning, the water and earth elements are increasing and these bring a tendency to heaviness and dullness unless they are counteracted by movement. This is where "early to rise" comes in. If we stay in bed late, our minds can become dull and our bodies will feel sluggish. So even if we feel a little tired in the morning, it is not a good idea to have a "long lie-in" because it will be counter-productive. Am I saying we should get out of bed at six? No, but if we have a habit of rising at a reasonable hour seven days a week, we will feel the benefits. Some people deprive themselves of sufficient good sleep when they are working and then try to make up for it at weekends but that's not so good. The body doesn't know where it is and staying in bed after 8 a.m. is going to reduce our sense of well-being.

If we can allow the body to harmonise with its natural cycles, we will be helping the growth of happiness. Going to bed between 10 p.m. and 11 p.m., and rising some time between 6 and 7.30 a.m. does just that and, if you do it already, you know!

(c) Exercise

Whatever the latest advice on exercise may be (and it does seem to change every couple of years) we should respect the cycles that affect our body. The water and earth elements have a tendency to make us heavier and the movement created by exercise, which increases the air element, brings lightness. It makes sense, then, to exercise more vigorously when water and earth are predominant. If we exercise too vigorously when air is predominant, air becomes too strong. An over-balanced air element increases the tendency to aging, dryness and brittleness; the body then becomes too light in character which makes it difficult to relax or settle. It may feel as though we are "on a high" at first but the nervous system will suffer and can become jittery if the imbalance continues. Of greater significance is the fact that the body's subtle energies are easily upset by too strong an air element and illness can eventually result; oriental medicine regards it as one of the most serious imbalances if allowed to continue.

So we should try to make our exercise fit in with the natural cycles if possible: reasonably vigorous when earth and water predominate, light when air predominates and moderate to light when fire predominates (because the body heats up easily). Earth and water are normally strong in late winter and in spring when the weather is colder and wetter; air is normally stronger in the autumn when the weather has a tendency to be windy and perhaps dry, and fire is at its strongest during high summer.

There is another cycle, though, that has a significant impact and that is the pattern of the elements in the life cycle. From childhood to old age there is a sequence that reflects nature. As children, we have a preponderance of earth and water because these are the elements that support growth. Frequent runny noses and much mucus are unfortunate evidence of this! Nature gives children lots of energy, and plenty of exercise is necessary to balance the heavier elements and to shape them. In adulthood, the fire element increases. The time of the "prime of life" is a period when the reproductive urge is strong, careers are made, families formed and so on. It should be an active and creative period which is encouraged by fire. At this time, exercise should be moderated from the vigour of childhood and adolescent exuberance but, assuming health is otherwise good, should still be reasonably demanding.

As we progress through adulthood, the air element gradually increases and this is when we need to be more careful. As we age, the skin tends to be a little drier, sleep is often lighter and often the appetite is less. Remember that the more vigorous the exercise, the greater the presence of the air element which can give rise to lightness in the nervous system. On the other hand, if we see that as a reason to sit down and laze around, we will start to develop inertia or dullness and our muscles and skeletal structure will weaken. At any age, exercise is necessary and makes us feel better. The trouble is that, as we age, we still feel young inside and forget that the body is changing. There will always be exceptions to the rule; there will always be men and women of advanced years who are able to run the London marathon and perform other feats of great endurance. Such people have extraordinary determination and they also have exceptionally strong bodies. Good luck to them, they're terrific. For most of us ordinary mortals, though, moderation in all things is generally sound advice and we will feel better if we support the body as it ages rather than hammer it into submission.

Once we pass the age of forty, exercise should normally be kept at a moderate level until by the age of seventy and beyond we are better with regular light exercise. Over-exercise in the sense of too much exertion when we are in middle age can actually increase the aging process rather than reduce it. Listen to your body; it will let you know when you are not doing enough or are doing too much, if you listen to it with honesty and openness.

Caring for our mind: suggestions for regular meditation

It is crucial to care for both the body and the mind. Neglect one and the other will suffer. The Chinese use the terms *yin* and *yang* to describe states of energy. In very broad terms, *yin* is when the energy is coming inwards; activity is less, conditions are colder, things are contracting. If something is too *yin*, inertia and dullness can set in. Conversely, *yang* is when the energy is outgoing; there is more activity, conditions can be hotter and there is a tendency to expansion. If something is too *yang*, there is too much activity and the energy becomes depleted quickly. *Yin* and *yang* are neither good nor bad. What the Chinese have understood for thousands of years is that it is important to balance the two states in order to attain equilibrium, whether that is in mind or body. Modern society creates conditions where it is easy for the body to be too *yin* due to insufficient physical activity and for the mind to be too *yang* due to incessant stimulus.

Daily meditation is an excellent way to balance the *yang* tendency of the mind. In chapter 5 we looked at some simple meditations for calming the mind and any of these will produce excellent effects if practised on a regular basis. For someone who has not meditated before, daily meditation may seem a tall order but millions of busy people manage it with little difficulty and, like saving money, the more you put in, the more you get out. The important thing is to really want to have a calmer, clearer mind and then decide that you will do something about it. Then simply do it! Having a genuine intention can be life-changing and regular meditation *is* life-changing. If you forget to do it or cannot fit it in one day, don't beat yourself up about it; tomorrow will be fine and you will do it then.

Traditionally, the best time to meditate is before breakfast when the body is rested after a night's sleep. It gives the best start to the day because we begin with a calm mind. Ten minutes is ample for beginners and if you haven't got ten minutes, think if it might be possible to get up a few minutes earlier. Some people, especially busy parents with children demanding attention from an early time may say it's impossible. Children can adjust to change but if it really is a non-starter, then any time in the day is good.

The second traditionally good time for meditation is at the end of the working day because it refreshes us from the arduousness of the day and gives us energy for the evening. When we meditate, though, is not crucial. What is important is that we find a time that suits our lifestyle best and try to stick to it if we can as regularity brings the greatest benefits.

Meditation once or twice a day for ten minutes each time will bring very noticeable changes. After a month or two of regular practice, an extra five minutes can be added if we are comfortable with the meditation process. If you think you need to do longer periods, it would be better to join a meditation class with an experienced teacher.

Coming out of any meditation slowly is really important because the body can come to quite a deep level of rest. If we come out too quickly it could jar the nervous system which could leave us feeling a little uncomfortable. Allow a couple of minutes to come out slowly.

Decide before you start how long you are going to do rather than finish when you feel you have had enough. Sometimes the mind or the body can feel a little restless in meditation and you may feel tempted to stop and get up. Symptoms of restlessness are just signs that some stress or tension is being released so just stay with it, be easy and it will pass. How do we know when to end the meditation? Using a timer that bleeps is not a good idea because it can make us jump. It is far better to have a watch or small clock close by; when you think it might be time, just take a little peek. If it's time to finish, close the eyes again and give yourself a couple of minutes to come out; if not, close the eyes and carry on. It won't be long before you know the time without looking.

For beginners, the simplest, easiest and most effective meditation to do without going to a meditation class is awareness of breath, sometimes called "quiet sitting", which we looked at in chapter 5. Here it is again:

- *Sit up reasonably straight with the hands resting in the lap or on the knees or thighs. If you are sitting in a chair, make sure that the legs aren't crossed at the knees and the feet are flat on the floor. It's important to be comfortable but if we slouch, we constrict the energy channels in the body, especially in the back, and we won't have the same benefit.*

- *Place the awareness on the lower abdomen and exhale, feeling the movement of the abdomen.*

- *Close the eyes and continue to breathe normally, simply being aware of the movements that come with the breathing.*
- *Thoughts will come in and wander out, just as clouds will float across the sky. Don't mind them and don't try to force them out; simply bring the awareness back to the lower abdomen and the breath.*

Meditation is not difficult. The only effort we really need to make is to sit down and do it. Most people are amazed how wonderful a calm mind is and how it can be achieved without experience or knowledge. Always sit with a "beginner's mind" – that is to say, be open and without expectation – and the mind will settle in its own time. Sometimes we will have a meditation that is filled with thoughts and then we might think that we are not meditating properly; this is perfectly normal but we are probably doing it correctly. Remember that the purpose of meditation is not simply for the ten minutes that we do it but for the other twenty-three hours and fifty minutes of the day. Meditation is about improving the quality of life and regular practice will do just that.

Managing ourselves when we are sick

It might seem odd to mention sickness in a book about happiness. A positive outlook on life does, without doubt, strengthen the immune system and happier people are generally healthier people. The truth is, though, that no matter how positive we are, at some time or another, the body will fall sick. Yet it can happen that a person with a positive, generally healthy outlook will actually deny sickness when it strikes and then a conflict arises in the mind. That conflict disturbs the happy equilibrium because deep down the person knows that he or she is in denial and also knows, or perhaps fears, that sickness is there after all.

Being happy involves an attitude of acceptance of whatever life brings. That doesn't mean we have to accept all conditions as acceptable, contradictory though that statement sounds. It means accepting that present conditions are as they are. If they need changing and we can change them, so be it, get on with it. But if the conditions are something that we can do nothing about, then there is no point in worrying. As we looked at in chapter 6, all conditions change in time; no condition is permanent.

Some people at the first sign of a common cold fear it. They take all sorts of concoctions to keep the "dreaded lurgy" at bay. Yet the cold isn't the issue. The real issue is the fear of the cold. People with happier minds succumb to colds far less often and as and when they do occur, the passage of the cold is generally swift and comparatively light. The fear of a cold (or of any other type of sickness) creates tension in the mind and consequently in the vital body. The fear weakens the immune system by making the vital body weaker. Crazy, isn't it? But it's true. The thing we fear, we make worse or create by fearing it.

Similarly, if in our minds we "fight" the disease, we tighten the body's defence systems when what we need to do is assist the body by increasing its ability to circulate the vital energy. The body falls sick because of an imbalance in the energy system and the way to overcome sickness is to restore balance. When the mind is in a happy state, when we are expressing positive emotions and when we smile, the channels in the vital body dilate and allow more energy to circulate, so allowing any imbalance to be restored more easily.

Although this is not a book on healing (or perhaps it is!) it is important to understand that all healing takes place from within. It may be necessary to have treatment, take medicines and so on but any external agent or any healer, whether orthodox or otherwise, can only and does only provide the necessary conditions to enable the healing process to take effect within the patient. Our role, when we are sick, is to cooperate with the inner healing process and that cooperation cannot happen if we are tense.

If self-management during time of sickness means cooperating with the healing process, what can we actually do?

- *Accept* that things are as they are. Symptoms are the body's signal that it is trying to right itself and that it is in healing mode.

- *Don't focus* on the symptoms. Self-indulgence is not required and often leads to a "poor me" syndrome which is a negative state of mind. Health is a matter of radiance; "poor me" leads to the opposite.

- *Relax and rest* as much as possible as the body uses up more energy when healing is in progress and disturbances in energy can settle more easily when there is rest. If we still have to work, it is better to try to use less energy and avoid becoming overtired. Remember that tension interferes with healing so relax and let go often. By the same token, try to go to bed early; the body will be most grateful for it.

- *Smile to your body.* This may sound a little odd but smiling to the body increases the flow of vital energy and makes us feel better. In a sense we bless the body when we do this and we can do it to the whole body or gradually work through the body from head to toe, smiling to or blessing each part.

- *Listen to your body more.* The body actually knows what it needs. As your awareness increases, you will find that by listening to your body you will know what it wants, whether it is a question of diet, exercise, rest, fresh air or something else.

- *Take appropriate medical advice.* Many people unnecessarily bother their physicians with minor ailments but there are many, too, who don't go to see them when they should and suffer as a result. If you think you need medical help, go and get it; if you are in doubt, go and get it.

Cultivating confidence and faith in ourselves

Lack of confidence, lack of faith, lack of self-esteem: these three bedfellows conspire to undermine any sense of happiness we may have. They are the source of stress, a great many ills, wrong thinking and illogical behaviour. They all arise from a basic state of ignorance where we think that there is a "me" to protect and if we think there is a "me" to protect, it also means that at some level we perceive a threat. That perception of threat gives rise to fear and, whether we care to admit it or not, we all possess fear in one form or another.

The steps we have looked at in this book will, if taken together, start to eliminate fear. Gradually a sense of confidence will increase as we become happier and delve into our true nature, which is boundless, radiant, blissful and unshakeable. Sometimes, though, something happens on this long path that reminds us that we haven't yet eliminated all fear and we find that our equanimity is disturbed. Then we don't think quite as clearly as we should and our reactions are not as they would normally be. A part of life suddenly seems a little, or perhaps greatly, stressful. Quite possibly we will blame the circumstances themselves because, after all, it is normal human reaction to want to find fault and then to make sure that that fault doesn't attach to this "me" we created. But really the immediate cause is a lack of confidence in ourselves, an inability to see that whatever life throws at us, we can and will cope, that our true nature, which lies beyond our name, our lifestyle and all things that contribute to our self-identity, is completely and utterly invincible.

There are numerous books, self-help programmes and the like which can help to boost self-confidence. What many ignore, though, is the state of the body's energy. If our energy is strong, our confidence will be strong also and conversely if our energy is weak and all over the place, our mind and self-perception will be weaker. An in-depth study of the body's energy beyond the scope this book but there is a simple exercise that can help very much to "strengthen our base". It features strongly in both tai chi and in chi kung. It can be done by anyone who can stand and if you are unable to stand for any length of time, it can be adapted: simply sit as upright as you can and proceed from the second "bullet point" below. Here it is:

- *Stand with the feet shoulder width apart or even a couple of inches wider. Adjust the feet so that the toes point straight ahead of you and the feet are parallel to each other. (If you suffer from bad knees or hips you might not wish to do this in which case stand in a way that is comfortable to you.) Relax the knees so they are not "locked" straight. The weight should be evenly balanced.*

- *Straighten the back and then relax the shoulders so that they drop – they will look rounded, which is good for this. Tuck the chin in a little so that the neck is straight and feel as though you are suspended by a thread from the top of the head. Now turn the hands, which should be relaxed, so that the palms face backwards and are slightly out from the side of the body. All this is the outer position.*

- *Now for the inner position. Place the tip of the tongue just behind the front teeth. Relax the abdomen and try to relax the perineum also (the perineum is the underside of the torso, between the genitals and the anus – or as I often say, "Where the bicycle saddle goes!") The gaze should be horizontal, as if you were looking out to a distant horizon.*

- *Breathe so that as you inhale the diaphragm comes down and pushes the abdomen out slightly and when you exhale the abdomen relaxes inwards a little.*

- *Allow the energy in the body to settle. Feel as if your energy is sinking downwards and that as it does, your mind empties.*

- *Bring your awareness to the soles of the feet and feel the contact with the floor. After a few moments, bring the awareness to the lower abdomen – below the navel – and feel as though your energy is becoming stronger there. Sometimes feel the feet, sometimes the lower abdomen and sometimes to the hands, but always come back to the lower abdomen as it moves with the breath.*

- *Feel as though you are very tall, very strong, and unshakeable. Remain standing in this way for 2, 3 or even 4 minutes.*

- *Finally, place the hands, one on top of the other, over the "lower dan tian" point (about three finger-widths below the navel) and take three or four deep breaths.*

Don't underestimate the effectiveness of this simple exercise. With just a little practice, it can build up resoluteness and a feeling of both inner and outer strength as the chi or vital energy becomes more stable and stronger in the lower part of the body. Whereas when our self-confidence is low we feel disconnected somehow, this exercise connects us mentally and energetically to the Earth and our surroundings, calms the mind and pacifies the nervous system.

How to just be and let go – responsibly

As you will have picked up from this book and almost certainly were already aware of instinctively if not consciously, happiness derives from an ability to let go. Discontentment and unhappiness are simply states of mind that arise from mistaken thinking. Please don't misunderstand me; I'm not saying that unhappy states of mind can't be exceedingly complex – they can and often are – but however complex and convoluted they may be, there is at their root a failing to let go. Your nature and my nature are, or I should say "is", one and the same: pure boundlessness. If we can experience who we *really* are in every given moment, happiness is inevitable. We simply need to be. It is only our inability, or rather unwillingness, to let go that prevents us from experiencing our own nature.

Letting go applies to many things and can mean different things to different people; and because we all hold onto so many different things, ideals, beliefs and concepts, it obviously isn't possible to let go of everything at once. Indeed, letting go is a lifetime's work. But the more we turn towards the idea of letting go, the more we surrender to the stream of life and the happier we become. So we could say that letting go is an attitude or an outlook on life rather than an end result.

How can we let go? *Simply relax and enjoy the present moment.* That's all there is to it: relax and enjoy the present moment. Be grateful for whatever the present circumstances are. When circumstances seem unfavourable, it means we have the opportunity to grow or to become stronger through whatever the situation is. So, right this minute, please – enjoy the present moment and be grateful for it.

Ambition can be good but it can also lead us into situations that eventually we do not want. Some people have found that letting go has involved giving up or changing a career, status or income. Only they know if that's right. Running away from things isn't good but sometimes a change is. Please relax and enjoy wherever you are sitting right now. Can you? If not, look at what you are hanging onto.

Letting go doesn't involve giving up responsibility but if responsibility is irksome, it may be our attitude towards it that is in error. On the other hand, if we have taken on extra responsibility because of the status or recognition it brings, perhaps we should look towards relinquishing it at some stage.

Simply relax and enjoy the present moment. That does not mean be a drop-out. Letting go does not involve abdication of responsibility. Everyone has a role in life and we should fulfil that role as best we can. Enjoying the present moment brings dynamism to what we have to do and gives us energy, not the reverse.

When emotions rise up, whether desire, anger, jealousy, pride or anything else, ask yourself this: "What am I holding onto?" Be easy; let go. These emotions aren't you; they arise like a wall in front of you obscuring your view or like a warped window, distorting everything you see. Let go and the emotions will settle again.

Regard yourself as owning nothing. Any property or money that you have, think in terms of it as having been lent to you by the Universe to look after and manage for a while. Even your body is lent to you. Everything has to be handed back at some point. Be attached to nothing but respect and care for everything. This is important.

Don't entertain worry. Worrying just wastes energy. Worrying happens when we fear what the future might bring. If you cannot do anything about the outcome, there's no point in worrying, so relax. You've survived everything life has thrown at you so far. If you can do something about the outcome, there's no point in worrying either, because you can prevent whatever it is you are worrying about.

Do your duties, whatever they may be, and enjoy life. When you find life is not enjoyable, if you look you will find tension in the body somewhere and some grasping in the mind. That isn't you. Let go of whatever it is and find yourself in the present moment because you are nowhere else to be found.

Simply relax and enjoy the present moment. There is only ever right now. Allow life to fill you and be fulfilled, now.

Thank you for reading this book. May you have a long life and be blessed with happiness and the causes of happiness. May you be filled with joy always and be free of suffering and all causes of suffering. May your heart always be peaceful.